Annie **Mack**

BadAss Pix

with a Cheap-Ass Camera

ISBN: 978-1-7354135-2-5

Published by Cresting Wave Publishing, LLC

"You Buy a Book, We Plant a Tree!"

Edited by Kris Neely

Layout by Kris Neely and Lazar Kackarovski

Photography and Photographic Descriptions by Annie Mack

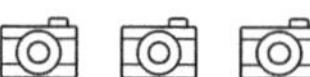

Front Cover left: "What Your Mind Does (When You're Not Watching)" (2016) Car manufacturers of the 1950s used wicked exterior paints. Practically indestructible and probably toxic as hell, but when they finally deteriorate it's so glorious it'll make you weep.

Front Cover, right: "Glacier Mountain" (2019) I am in eternal debt to the folks who invented Bondo, and for motorists who smash up their fenders and trowel in some Bondo to make it all better. Indeed, WAY better.

Back Cover, left: "Bad Moon Rising" (2018) Lightnin', hurricanes, rivers overflowing, voice of rage 'n ruin? Check, check, check, check, and check. All here!

Back Cover, right: "Stratocaster Live" (2015) An orbital sander gone haywire recreates the wild abandon and furious energy of a heavy-metal concert.

CONTENTS

ACKNOWLEDGEMENTS

Many thanks and much appreciation to these people for contributing to the creation of this project.

Mike Hoover and Vanessa Hadady, for the Badass title and professional encouragement, assistance, critique, and valued friendship.

Bill Pugh, for a rich education in darkroom, execution, composition, and imagination.

Paula Bautista, John Dooley, Paloma Dooley, Mo Dooley, and Melanie B. McFarland, for decades of fantastic opportunities and love to back them up.

Ann and John Christensen, forever inspiring, patient, hospitable, nudging when needed, and loads of fun.

Kyle Moore, for the Badass nickname and support of the creative process for many years in many settings.

Justin Grant, much thanks for the great big mat cutter and entree to the garage — where the magic happens.

Kate Smith, for being an enthusiastic partner in photographic crime.

Stacy Sims, for invites and expertise in many media.

Deborah Bunger, for showing me around Chicago and making the driver wait until I'd finished the Goose shot.

Kris and Laura Neely, for all you do, did, and done did.

My Instagram tribes and comrades, for sharing wonderment and ideas.

Jessica Fong, Maria Flumiari, Denny Ah-Tye, Charlene Warren Martin, JC Strote, Caroline Henry, Darrell O'Sullivan, Vicki Gaia, Jim Melquist, and all the denizens of the Stockton Art League and the Lodi Community Art Center, for training, suggestions, information, use of space, and valuable connections.

The Girls' Afternoon Out Gals: Chrys, Lisa, Deb, Stacy, Terri, Bird, Allison, Franca, and more. For lively discussions and loyal attendance at shows, galas, and other exhibitions.

Robin Ringstad, Ed Auerbach, Khira and Taryn Auerbach, for food for thought and the belly.

Becky Ponce, for art appreciation, amazing vision, and being too dangerous for our own good when we get together.

Special love and thanks to Walt and Evan Freeman for too many reasons to list, but primarily for waiting in the car; posing for holiday-card pictures; assisting with construction, carpentry, ladders, moving, or lifting heavy objects; financing of said activities; and understanding.

And extra appreciation to Evan for 24/7/365 tech support and keeping the hardware and software up to date and almost nearly within my skill range.

Annie

FOREWORD

Disclaimer: It has been an immense pleasure to know Annie Mack since we were in High School together a whole passel of U.S. Presidents ago.

To know her is to know someone funny, smart, irreverent, as serious as they get, hard-working, a dedicated activist, fiercely loyal to her tribe — and one Hell of a photoartist with a cheap-ass camera in her hands.

It is an honor to bring some of Annie's work to the public eye.

When my wife and I founded Cresting Wave Publishing, we wrote a list of the types of books we wanted to publish and the ones we thought we would take a pass on. Yep - books centered on photographs were on the "Naw. Thanks anyway" list.

That is, right up to the moment we first glimpsed Annie's work. To me, her work has a Zen-like quality to it.

Look: then... *see*. Observe: but *do not* classify. Experience for yourself: not as you think someone else would want you to.

And when you have experienced this book of Annie's art, I am hoping you could do me a personal favor: tell three other people about the work, the art, and the vision of Annie Mack. I know they will thank you, as I do. Thank you.

Kris Neely

Co-Founder, Cresting Wave Publishing
Spokane, Washington, Late Winter, 2021

THE
WORDS

BADASS PICTURES WITH **A CHEAP-ASS CAMERA**

What are Badass Pix?
Basically, photos. But not just any photos.
Let me tell you what they're not.

Photography can be a lot of things. The things it usually is, without splitting the entire discipline down to the molecular level, are photojournalism, scenic photography, and portraiture.

- Photojournalism is freezing a real moment in time that is a piece of a larger story. The photographer should be impersonal and objective yet woke enough to recognize context and use an image to tell a bigger story. AKA event or sports photography.
- Scenic photography means going to an exceptionally gorgeous place with unbelievable natural features or architecture and recording the image to bring it back to the unlucky people who aren't there.
- Portraiture is making an image of a person or people who likely has/have paid the camera operator to make him/her/them look handsome or pretty, even if it involves manipulation to the point of being unrecognizable. Also, capture the personality/character of the subjects, if any. See also: Fashion Photography.

Then, there are Badass Pix.

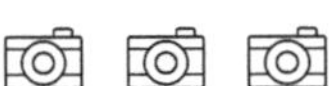

OK THEN, WHAT IS BADASS?

Badass is not a genre. It's an attitude, an approach, a vibe. More than anything, it's Art Photography, which is a h-u-g-e and diverse categorization. It's you being a photo***artist***, not just a photographer.

It's having the self-confidence to take risks, break the rules, and venture outside norms. It's rebellion! Anarchy! A fight for freedom! But you know: without jail time, a rap sheet, a prison tattoo, or stitches.

Badass can be photojournalism, scenery, portraits. It is fun to screw around with all of those and add twists that baffle viewers. Badass is futzing around outside the boundaries of technology, good taste, or conventional artistic theory. Badass uses your tools, skills, and heart to make Art — not just 'nice' photos.

Badass Pix are squinted at, disqualified from contests, or vaguely labeled "mixed media," "digital graphics," or "weird shit."

Most of the work I call Badass, illustrated here, is found-art photography, which more-or-less means art made by recording the image as one finds it. Simply...as is.

Now I can imagine you saying, "Well, duh, that's pretty much all photography, now isn't it?"

Not really: here's some help. Badass is trying to find images that most people miss or never see at all because it takes imagination (some might say awareness. Or both) to recognize them.

Deep, Heavy, Mostly Totally True Words:

GO FOR CREATIVITY, AND YOU'LL EVENTUALLY LEARN AS MUCH PRECISION AS YOU NEED.

I took some darkroom photography classes, where "serious" students were shooting for dazzling perfection of epic subjects. I was "that student" because I was chasing some intriguing quirky ideas, whether or not I could make 'em work. In the creative process, I figured out how to push the camera's buttons — and push other people's buttons.

It was, to coin a phrase, badassical.

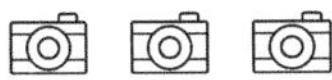

Some of these Badass Pix are abstracts. Abstraction is mostly assigned to painting, which involves the deconstruction (artists love that word) of a recognizable figure or object into chaos, nothingness, primary color, or no color. The painter wields the brush or palette knife and obliterates all specific details and leaves the emotional and spiritual essence splayed all over the canvas.

It looks easier than it is.

Merely flinging paint at the wall can make a lovely or horrid mess, but with no guarantee that it's meaningful or resonant.

Abstract photography is even more complicated because cameras are built to record with precision. It takes a will and a while to figure out how to dump imagery and spill pixels everywhere. Photographers shoot actual stuff, either formations or creatures they find in nature, or man-made junk they see in the street or the garage. Abstraction in photography is usually achieved through cropping or using a macro lens to distort and render the object unrecognizable, or — this is a real thing — using a faulty camera to break through the limits of reality. More on this later.

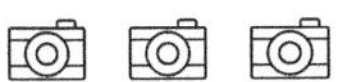

Back to the beginning: the three genres mentioned above are dependent on realism. Scenic photography is pretty much denotative and literal, meaning "what you see is what you get" of a mappable piece of real estate: the crest of a mountain against a glorious sunset, an aerial view of Red Square, and so on.

Photojournalism is shooting REAL people in REAL time. You can get into trouble for cropping, photoshopping, or distorting (i.e., taking a close shot to make the street crowd look like Yankee Stadium opening day when it's really a handful of shoppers who didn't even know there was a protest).

Portraiture is the replication of a REAL person at a specific moment. However, the use of make-up and Photoshop-ping to erase wrinkles and pimples can become fairly...unreal.

Well, you get the picture.

Realism demands rules.

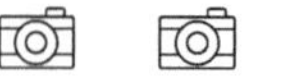

'DEM RULES

Shame on you if you mess up the majesty of Yosemite. Or pick a poor angle for the winning touchdown. Or fail to remove an icky zit.

To seek validation of their work, photographers enter competitions, which are constricted with oppressive rules. To wit, entries must be:

- framed, matted, glassed, and wired for hanging.
- shot within a specific time period.

- no larger than X, no smaller than Y.
- all recognizable persons must be named and have signed a release.
- no double-exposures or computer-generated images.
- ...and ad infinitum to death. (Or the wish that you were...)

In ancient times (...before 15 years ago), contests routinely required the photo to be relatively unretouched and uncropped. This one stipulation is not so much a thing in the digital age. That said, a winning entry is still often judged by how well the shot conforms to traditional expectations and highly technical standards.

I was in a show quite recently where the judge actually said the quality of the —- FRAME (yes, you read that right)—- swayed his choice. *Seriously?!?*

Anyway, back to the point: When a photographer is guided by the mandate to capture a classic "perfect" picture, he or she may achieve it, and it may well be beautiful, and it may well win prizes or sell.

Well...*clap clap clap*. It sure as Hell ain't no Badass, and it may be less art than you were shooting for.

Photo Clubs are big on that 'exactamento stuff,' which is why I don't recommend joining them — if you want to be Badass.

Photo Clubs, in theory, are supposed to "bring together folks who have a common interest in photography." My experience has been that the group, overall, is typically a friendly bunch, to be sure. But...there is always at least one lurking a Know-It-All who knows A-Lot-But-Not-As-Much-As-(S)he-Thinks, who seems to be the source of helpful advice — but really is a control freak who wants to cure you of divergent tendencies (read: your badassery).

This person will quietly — but insistently — mansplain (disclaimer: they mansplain regardless of gender) all the tiny details of numerical camera settings and theorems of geometry that will ensure optimum triangulation of camera, light, and subject. Essential Knowledge Stuff, as they explain it.

Be polite. *Whatever!* But avoid him or her.

This person may have won a few prizes and probably has some cred but recognize what he/she's doing: showing off, feeding their ego, or (more likely) trying to keep you from bringing "horrible" stuff to the show-and-tell part of the meetings. It's fun to win (yeah!) but winning or doing things the "right way" is not, and perhaps should not, be the driving force of every photoartist.

Deep, Heavy, Mostly Totally True Words:

DON'T GET HUNG UP ON TECHNICAL MINUTIAE
OR MAINSTREAM NORMS. FEED YOUR CREATIVITY INSTEAD.

Even Annie Liebowitz (my personal heroine and a ***Black Belt Badass***) laughs it off in her Master Class series, saying something to the effect of, "Which lens are we using today?"

Ha!

I want to be **that** Annie. *Artist Annie.*

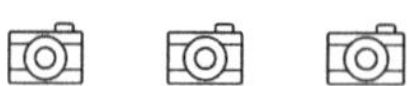

MR. CONNOTATIVE MEET MS. FIGURATIVE

As opposed to being precise and straightforward, Badass Pix are often connotative and figurative. They find symbols, metaphors, and visual innuendo to create a critical thinking puzzle for the viewer. The angles or viewpoints can and quite often do distort reality and disguise identity.

Badass Pix move away from conventional photography's expectations. But this movement is not for mere novelty's sake or to show what sort of undecipherable images a picture-taking machine can generate. No. Rather, the "Prime Directive" of Badass Pix is to make you, the viewer, speak art; to make you, the viewer, see art; and to make you, the viewer, ***feel*** art - all at once, in the *first* glance, before the *first* blink.

Now to be fair — at said first glance, you may be wholly confuzzled (to put it mildly) by whatever it is this crazy photographer is pointing a camera at. Stick around. This is ***precisely*** the goal of Badass: *to provoke the viewer to exert some creativity and imagination and think of their own!*

Badass Pixers use the camera as an artistic tool, just like paint, clay, wood, or all the above. Give that machine some respect! Regardless of its price, a camera is an elegant machine born to be more than just an obedient recorder. If you asked it (*Just go with me, OK? Quit being so literal...),* it would say it wants to get out and play like everyone else!

So...

Let. ➤ It. ➤ Run and Play. ➤ And run with it... ➤ Free in mind. ➤
➤ No limitations. ➤ No preconceptions. ➤ No rules. ➤ *See, feel, shoot.*

Be so wild-ass creative that your Badass Pix are too raw, too original, to be contained in a mere frame or mat. Badass Pix *should* push limits! Here's the formula:

Badass Art = (Heart * Your Own Artistic Authority).

Badass is about making art, not scoring a perfect 10.

Deep, Heavy, Mostly Totally True Words:

IF YOU CRAVE VALIDATION AND BASE YOUR SELF-WORTH ON PRIZES AND ACCOLADES, DON'T.

IT'S A TERRIBLE WAY TO LIVE AND YOU'LL BE DISAPPOINTED ALL THE TIME.

WHO. GIVES. A SHIT. WHAT. THE. SCORE. IS?

So, in case you were still wondering, this book will NOT teach you how to use your camera and equipment. Join a photo club (sorry, just kidding!). Download and read the manual for your damn camera — which, if you haven't noticed, is already way smarter than you when it comes to taking a photo even if ALL you do is just remove the lens cap, point the camera, push the button, and look at the picture! Even a cheap-ass camera gets busy adjusting focus, light exposure, shutter speed, and then starts beeping or jerking when you don't obey.

And don't sweat it: you will eventually learn about f-stops, ISO, depth of field, and how to tell your camera to F'off so you can try something different. Trust me: basic photography is *really* basic. Learn an essential photographic skill one-by-one, practice it a few times, and then just shut up and drive.

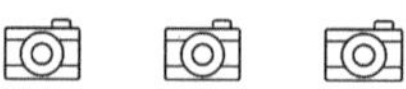

THE BADASS FINE PRINT

Now, Badass has a few rules too.

- An out-of-focus shot is usually just bad, not Badass.
- A choppy composition is just a hot mess, not Badass.
- The elements and principles of Design are handy helpers for ramping up a "Meh..." photo.
- Stoopid happens. Mistakes happen. But that ain't art, and it needs to be fixed, so the artist doesn't look the fool.
- On occasion, your Badass will get lucky by flinging out some "What the actual fuck?" junk and covering your momentary non-Badass by saying, "I meant to do that!" when you had no idea what just happened. Who said it wasn't...insight?
- But that knife cuts both ways: you also must recognize when shit is shit and challenge yourself to do better. Badass agitates for a reason.
- Badass shakes things up and disturbs the norms with purpose and intelligence.
- Badass is laser-focused and, like a laser, cuts through iron-clad reinforcements of excuses, lying, and just not giving a damn.
- Badass is keeping your art real. Period.

BAD TO THE BONE MEETS CHEAP TO THE END

Alright, we've beaten Badass to death. Time for some righteous Cheap-Ass.

Money isn't everything.

Money can't buy me love.

Back to being low-down honest: there's a good chance you are a broke-ass aspiring photographer. No problem. Rock on. So what? Welcome to the human race. That said:

You. ➤ Got. ➤ This.

You CAN create fantastic stuff with inexpensive and relatively simple tools. Learn to use your imagination, your inner sight, your eye — and the equipment will follow you.

To be sure, professional-grade photography is made with higher-end equipment. Not much argument there. Commercial standards value razor-sharp focus and saturated colors in recording actual items, scenes, and/or vain people who are terrified of exposing a double chin or a bad haircut. Complex, expensive cameras have functions and apps that can practically take the picture, drive the car home, run the shot through the computer, cook dinner and walk the dog.

Hey, we all drool over fancy technology. Imagine that someone gifts you a Hasselblad H6D-400c MS Medium Format DSLR Camera valued at $47,995.00... plus tax. In that case, you GRAB IT AND RUN (after you regain your ability to breathe and can pretend you didn't just have a mild heart attack.)

You own that your crummy point-n-shoots have limited scope and less mechanical ability. That's a fact too, but it's not the mic drop. Secret: really epic cameras are almost Idiot Savants. You know, like Rain Man in the movie, or Data on Star Trek, or (stretching), himself of Young Sheldon. Lots of knowledge, ability to do calculus and trigonometry from memory in two seconds but lagging in social skills and imagination. "Smart," but not always wise.

The ARTIST is more important than the stuff (s)he uses to make the art. Sure, the $48K Hasselblad can help your work look fantastic — as it damn well should. But a photo klutz without vision or basic compositional skills will be shot-shamed and outed by both the rattiest and the most awesome cameras money can buy.

Net-net: the artist makes the shot. The gear is necessary, but the price is irrelevant to a large degree, as we just saw.

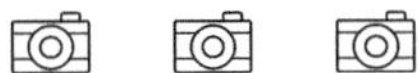

One exception to cheap-ass: a basic Photoshop-type app is vital, and you really can't fudge this. It doesn't have to be the freshest version. Essential functions for brightness/contrast, color, cropping, and cleanup will do for starters.

Most of my pieces were spiffed up with a near-Neanderthal prequel to Photoshop called "Picture It!", which was a free download I lucked upon once when I had film photos saved onto a CD at the drugstore. (*Yeah, yeah. None of that "OK Boomer" noise from you people in the back row.)*

Shooting the piece is the fun part.

The work part? Maybe not so orgasmic and thrilling. Often frustrating and sometimes psychotic insane is that — you must process art to get it to the viewers.

Like the tree that falls in the forest, but no one hears it: Is it *really* Art if nobody ever sees it but you? I have to say, "Sorta... No." You should not spend valuable time making art, only to become famous after you're dead because you kept said art hidden where no one could see it!

You do not need to own the equipment, at least not right away, but you could become friends with someone who's got at least a computer with some capability and a so-so printer.

No — you can't do everything on your phone. Not even the latest, most excellent, ten-minutes-ago version. And by-the-way, going electronic/digital/online is pivotal in snagging followers.

And, selling your stuff for almost-decent money (your mileage may vary on how you define "almost-decent"), but it's not the whole enchilada. At some point, the art will need to show up in some physical format.

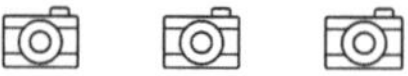

Hope for all of us schmucks: I made 99% of the BadAss Pix in this book with Cheap-Ass Cameras. Primarily, a $200 Canon point-and-shoot and a few iterations of iPhones (nothing more advanced than an iPhone 4 and an iPhone 6, when iPhone 10s and iPhone 11s were already out).

For eons, I processed them on a genuinely lousy laptop. Eventually, my tech-savvy computer-assembling exasperated son kidnapped it and built me a speedier, sleeker desktop. *(Thanks, Buddley.)*

Deep, Heavy, Mostly Totally True Words:

SAY IT AGAIN: FANCY EQUIPMENT IN UNSKILLED HANDS MIGHT FORGIVE A LACK OF EXPERTISE.

BUT A WELL- DEVELOPED ARTISTIC SENSE CAN MAKE COOL THINGS HAPPEN WITH INEXPENSIVE TOOLS.

And that's my point. Therefore, this book. Be an Artist! Explore! Play! Fall down, go boom, and get your ass up again!

Pack up whatever junk you have!

We gonna go be BadAss.

BADASS PICTURES WITH A CHEAP ASS CAMERA: **BASIC HARD-WON SUGGESTIONS**

(...WHICH MAY BE IGNORED OR MOCKED, BUT, HEY, AT LEAST THINK ABOUT THEM!)

F**ocus.** Use a camera setting that captures the subject sharply. And, please, as a personal favor to me, keep the damn lens clean! Blurry shots are rarely acceptable — even if intentional. Your audience hates to squint without resolution. They will drop you and your art like a bad habit if you can't pay enough attention to your craft to offer them a focused picture through a clean lens. A tripod is a good bargain. Hey, even the most basic tepee-of-metal-sticks models are helpful.

Focus. But in this sense, I mean have a focal point or subject in the shot. Incorporating excessive themes, hues, actions, or details is like hoarding junk to the point where you risk death by avalanche in your own home. More is not always better and pointless confusion is not genuine Badass disruption of the paradigm.

Get out. Of the house, that is. And of the neighborhood, of your comfort zone, of your head, and way the Hell out of self-censorship. Study art and photography (save time, realize you will never out-Yosemite Ansel Adams, but also see what's-been-done) and extrapolate. Learn to recognize remarkable. Oh, and one essential point here: yes, you can and perhaps should draw inspiration from another person's work. But DO NOT COPY.

Deep, Heavy, Mostly Totally True Words:

PLAGIARISM IS NOT ONLY NOT COOL,
BUT IT IS ALSO A CRIME.

The cheap publicity will only last until the gallery owner discards your work or you become entwined in a plagiarism argument that will drain you of valuable energy, time, and cash. A true artist's compass is originality and self-expression, not petty theft, or possession of stolen property (*also crimes!*)

Avoid gimmicks. Snapchat puppy-ears or sparkly stars are for social media, **not** the gallery. Kitschy topics (think Thomas Kinkade snow scenes with twinkly lights and glowing windows) may catch on for a while but soon (and sometimes not soon enough) turn into clichés. Less obvious but equally deadly are apps and filters that distort or superimpose a pattern; these become too predictable and boring after being applied only once or twice (think: those Rorschach fake-mirror image-makers or the kaleidoscope thingamajig in your phone). Even bigger picture: beware of becoming immersed in a "signature" look or branding element.

Deep, Heavy, Mostly Totally True Words:

IF VIEWERS AUTOMATICALLY YELL OUT, "THAT'S A [YOUR NAME]!",
YOU MAY BE GETTING... GIMMICKY.

Editing and processing. These skills are vital if you want to be taken seriously as an artist. Raw works can be edgy or arresting, but most need just a *little* polish to move up from amateurism. Color and contrast adjustment are standard refinement tools. Cropping and minor Photoshopping (removing dust specks, glare spots, obnoxious photobombers) are acceptable housekeeping tasks.

Next is presentation. Whether it's printing, matting, mounting, dangling, projecting, cyber sharing, or putting your work on coffee cups. Presentation can be the difference between enchanting the audience or turning them off with shoddy appearances. Again, you don't need to buy overpriced genuine-wood-look frames, but maybe you want to respect your work more than to tack a crumpled sheet of posterboard to the bathroom door. Just sayin'.

Have fun! A sense of humor, whether sly or over-the-top slapstick, is key to badassery. If you take yourself too seriously, you won't take enough risks. A silly slip or obvious boo-boo can lighten the mood and be the engine for a runaway train of thought. Explore a song title or an idiom, or fool around with puns, alternate images, or sight gags.

Shoot, shoot, shoot = practice, practice, practice. Get experience with general composition, shadows, lighting, speeds, and so on.

Deep, Heavy, Mostly Totally True Words:

LEARN BY DOING. THIS WILL HELP WEED OUT THE DULL AND UNREMARKABLE TOO.

Been-There-Done-That-Moment: If, after seventy-five snaps, the trees in fog or the strobe-lit concert haven't yet jumped off the page, they probably won't. Time to change up your angle, approach, settings, or intent.

Keep moving. Hopefully forward.

THE
ART

ART SECTION I: **REFLECTIONS**

This is often an early-on assignment in photo classes.

Everyone uses mirrors or puddles. An online "expert" assures us that Reflection Photography is terribly difficult and can ONLY be accomplished by professional photographers, who are the ONLY ones who get the ideas of viewpoint, angles, and "other factors" which were not mentioned.

When you quit laughing, let's mess with that.

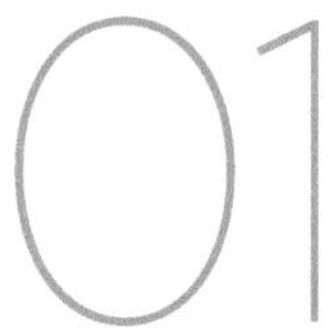

CHICAGO RIVER, 2011

The so-called "rule" is to stake out,

with fervent hope and TONS of free time,

that instant when the water is a miraculously perfect mirror...

...of your subject.

Yeah, right.

Movement and animals give the picture life. And I'mma tell the *goose* to get out the way? I was rooting for him!

"C'mon, Loosey! Swim into that pale quadrant! Please!"

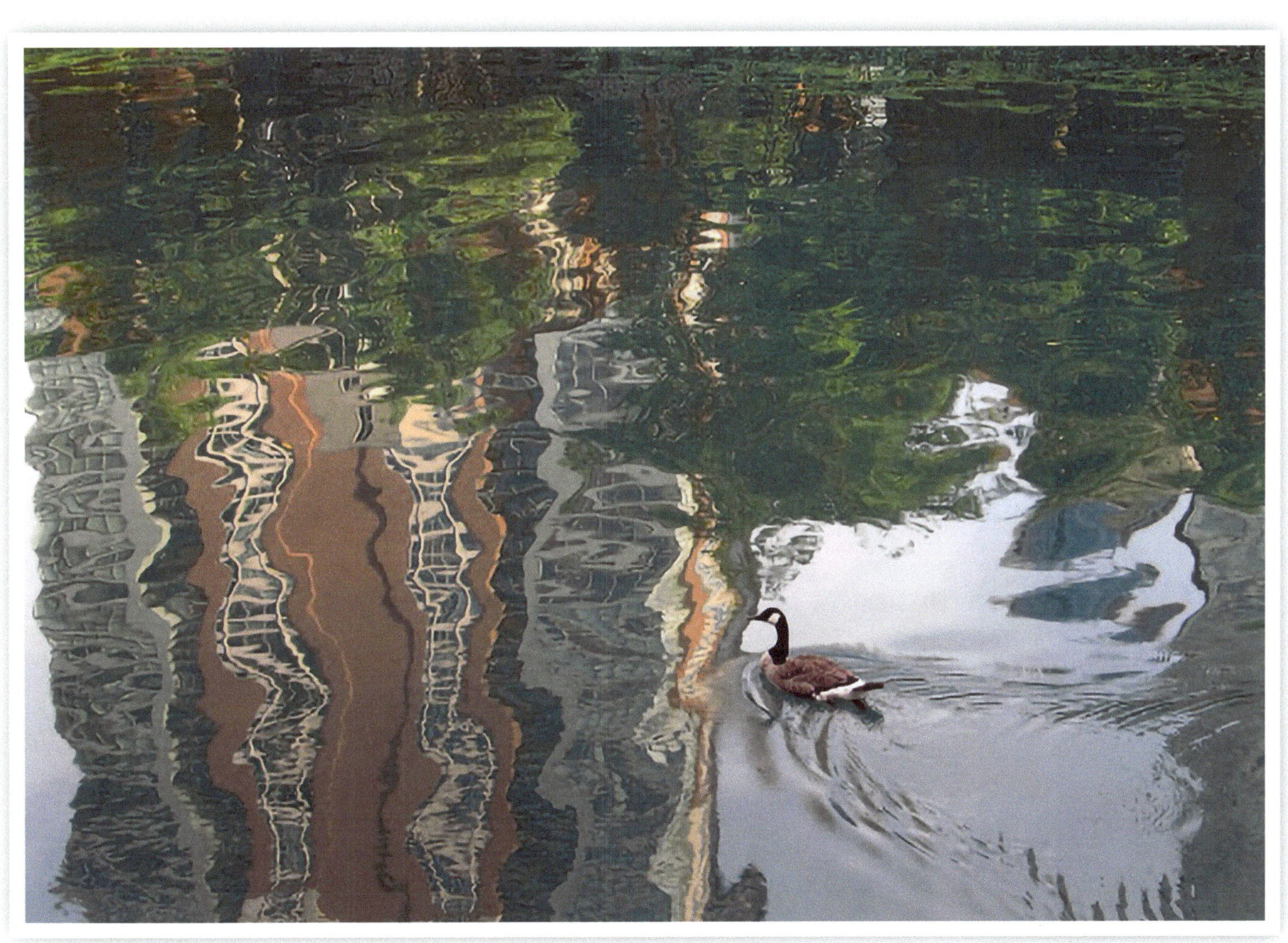

02

2ND STREET TUNNEL, 2014

A famous underpass in downtown Los Angeles. Almost every movie from the last 30 years that has a tunnel car-chase scene was filmed here.

I entered this picture in a newspaper photo contest.

A judge noted that while most folks aimed for “accurate visual representations,” I had pushed beyond into “artistic impressionism.”

Wise and a bit badass, he was.

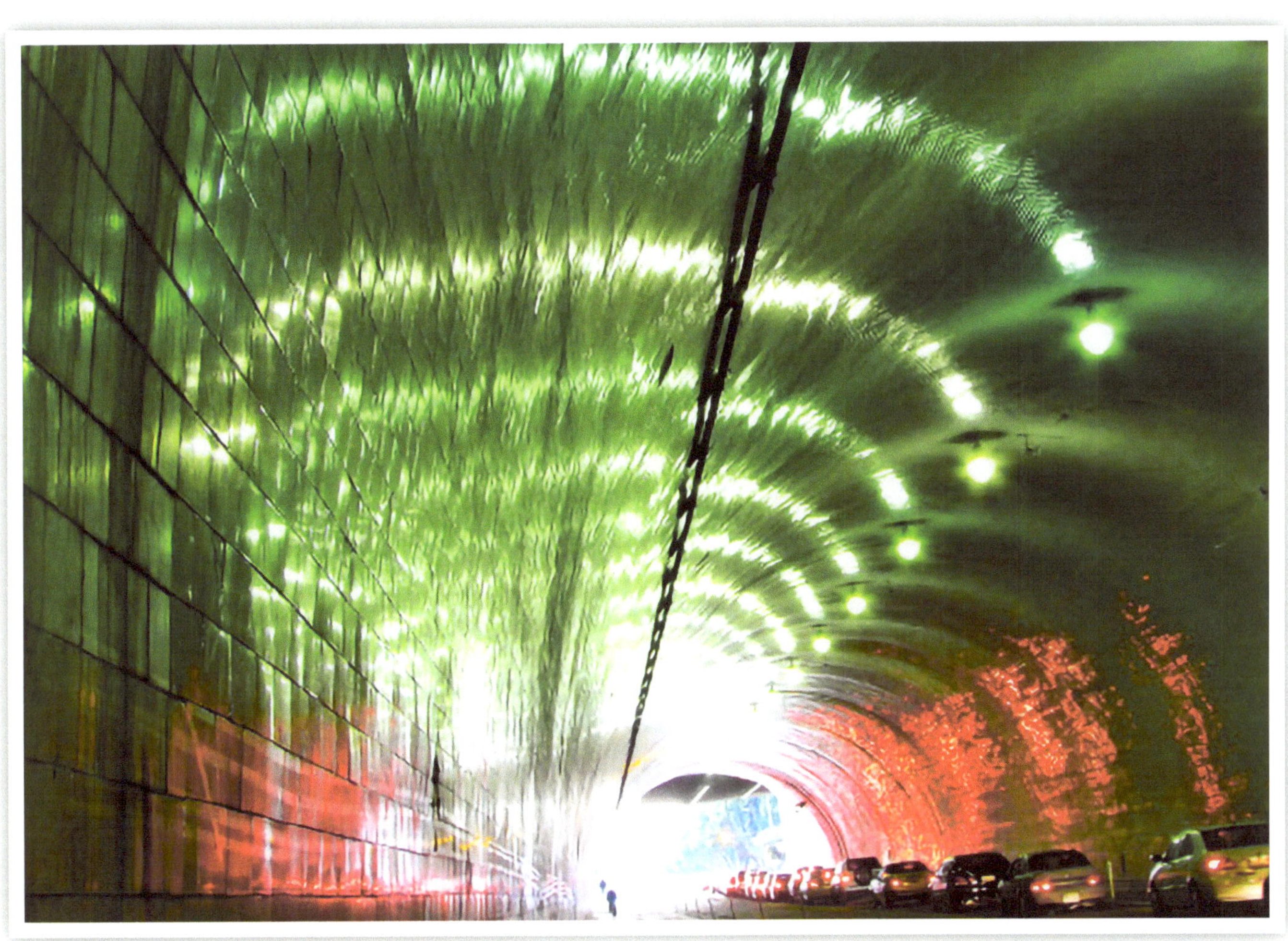

03

SELFIES, 2014

Two heads, three cameras, half a dozen hands.
What every photographer really needs!

This was shot at the Walt Disney Concert Hall of the Los Angeles Music Center, originally designed to have a stone exterior, but due to cost overruns, they went with a cheaper skin made of stainless steel plates.

Much better for capturing reflections, IMHO.

Note the cheap-ass camera!

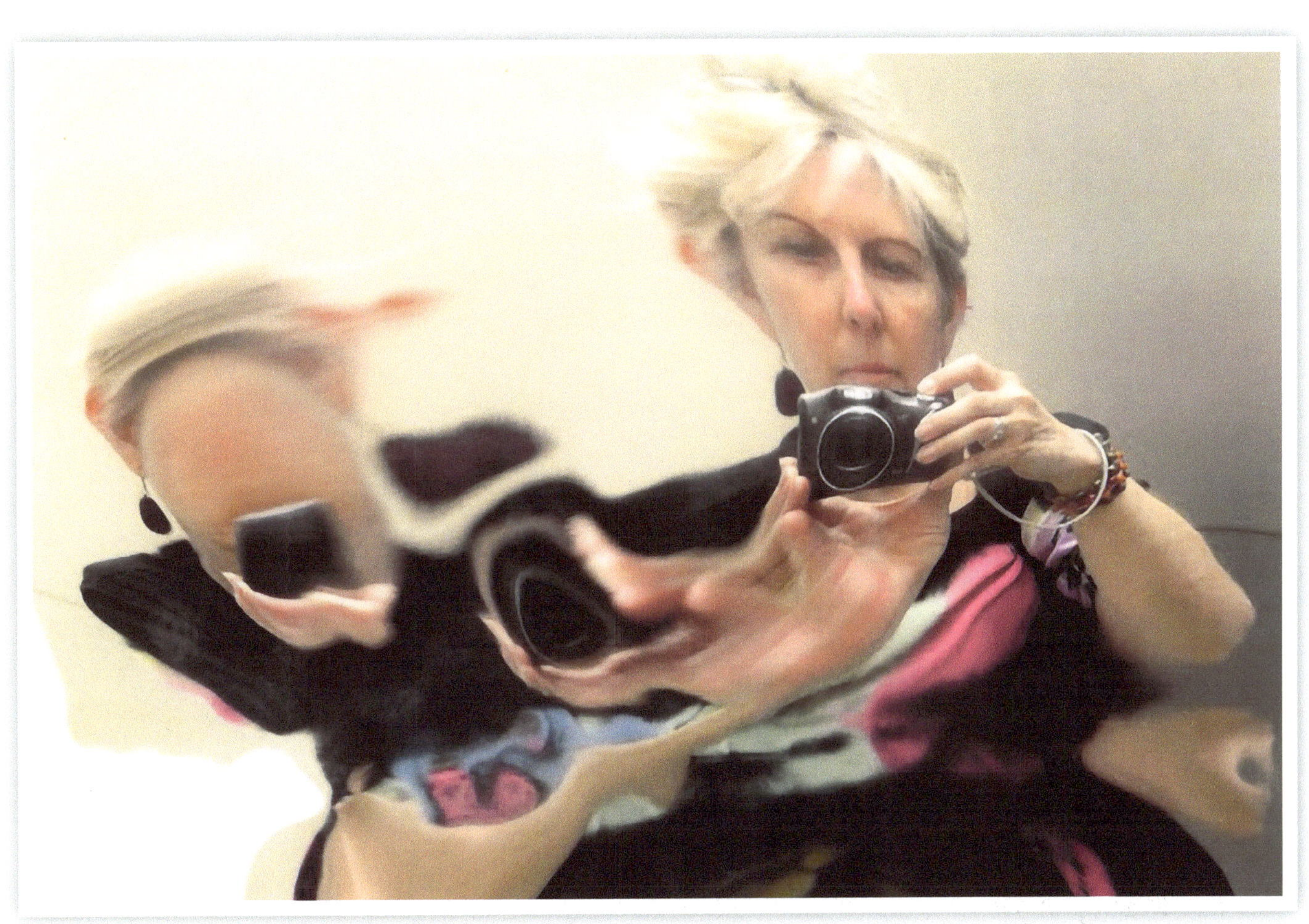

04

HOME IN SNOW, 2015

I arranged pieces...

of cardboard, fabric, and colored paper to reflect...

Imperfectly,

Onto a galvanized metal box.

This is a photo abstract, as there was never any home or snow. I tried to evoke the sensation of arriving at the safe and warm on a cold winter's night.

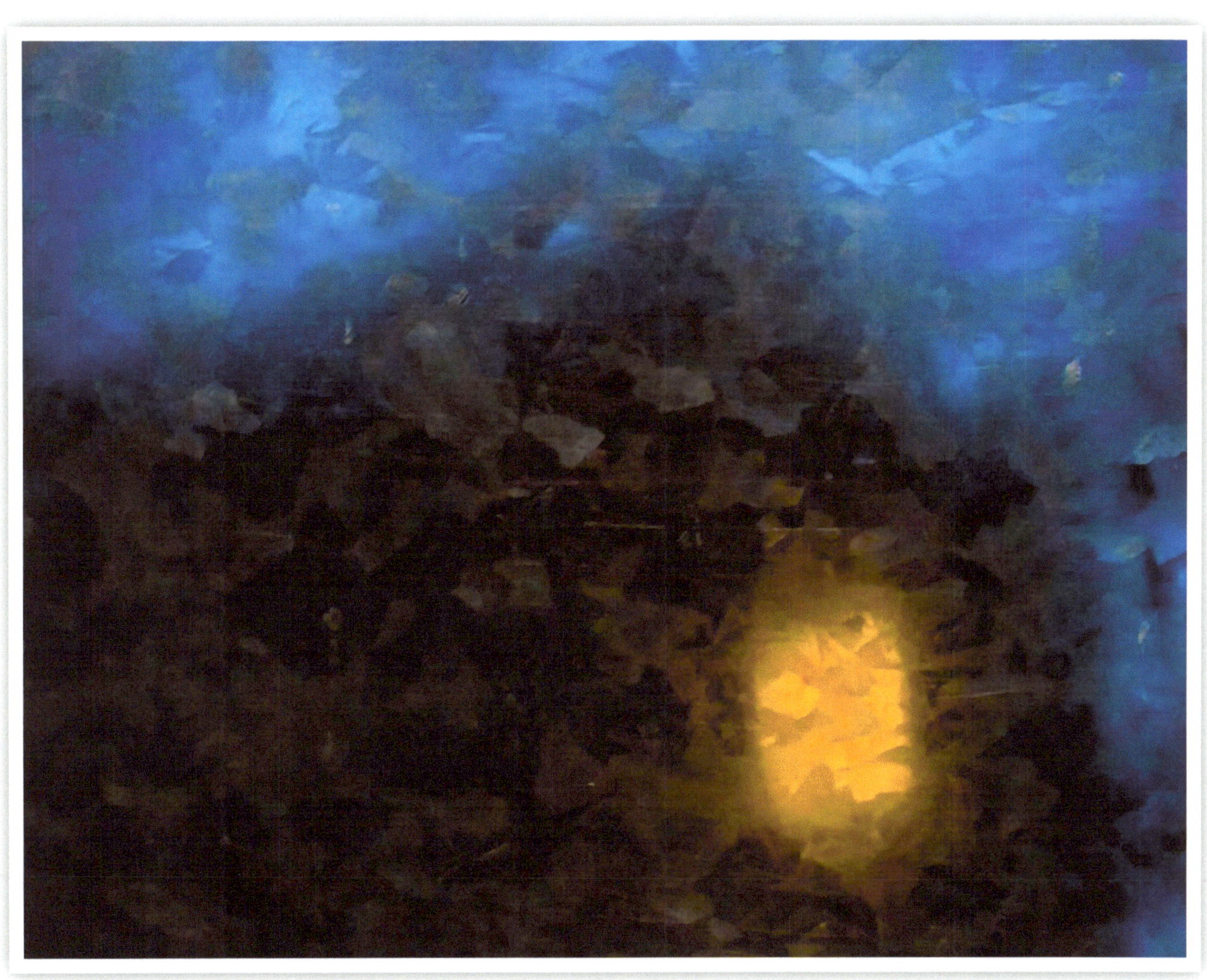

05

CHRYSLER BUILDING, 2008

It's reflected on the window-wall across the street.
The Happy Accidental Tourist...

...who wanders in the opposite direction of the rest of the busload.

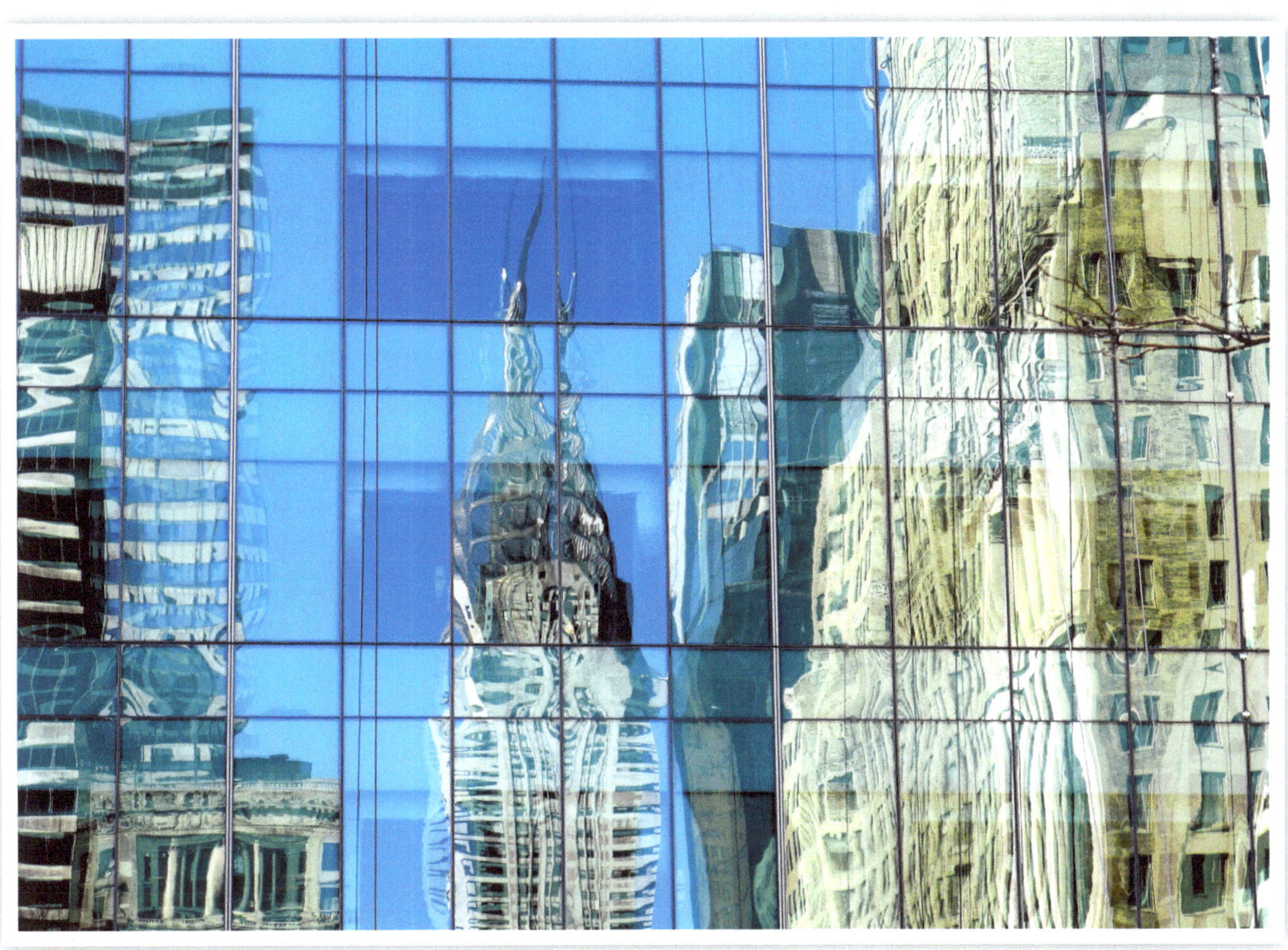

06

TACO TRUCK, 2011

One of my first iPhone triumphs.

I felt like a Cold War spy with a matchbook camera,
as I turned my back on the man...

...and shot at his reflection on the quilted-metal panel on the truck.

Stealth is an invaluable photographic skill.

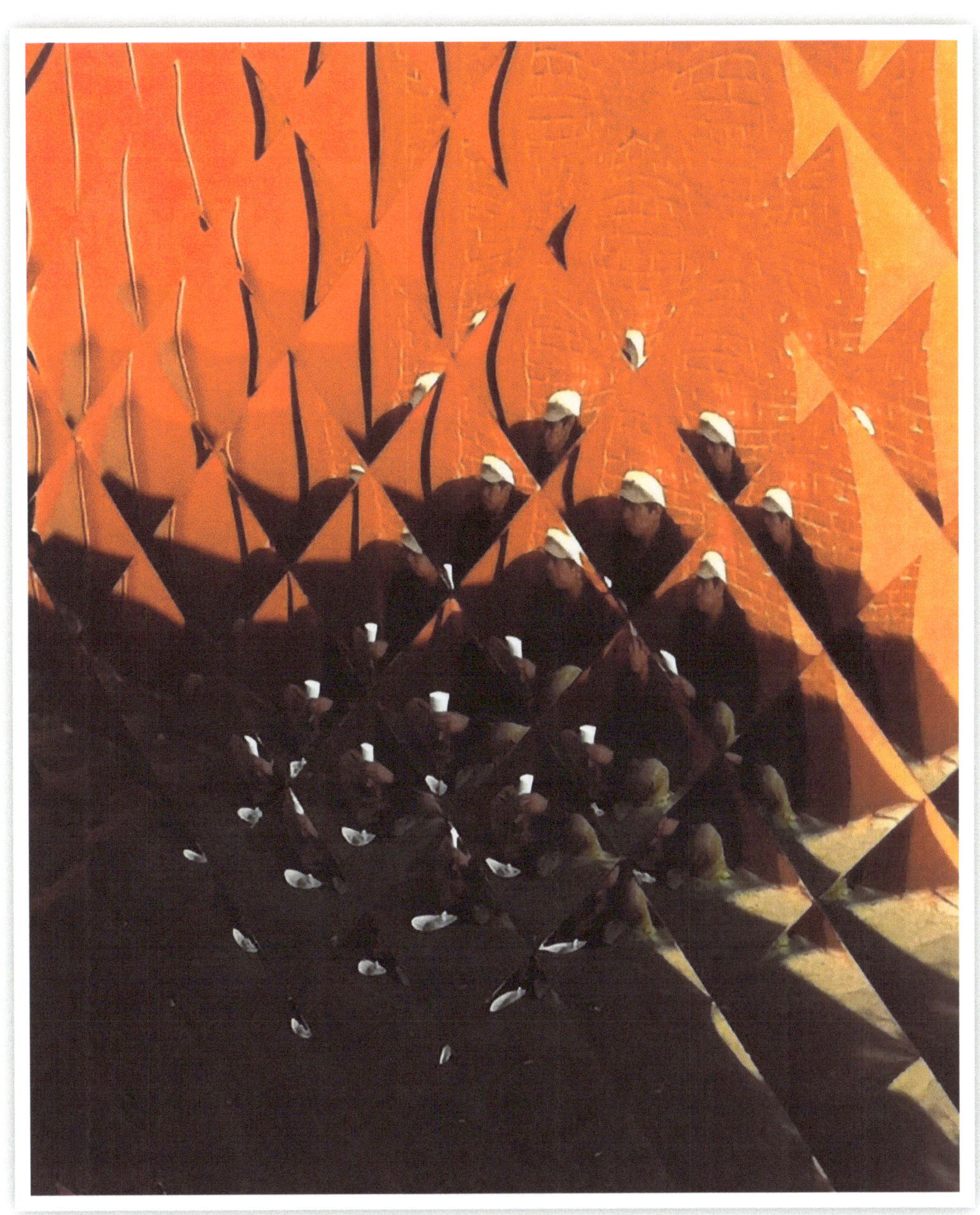

07

GIRL IN GOWN, 2007

This began as a quick find.

I pointed the camera at a glass block — you know, those transparent swirly brick-like chunks that they build into the wall at the dentist's office so light comes in but people on the sidewalk can't clearly view the agony of your root canal.

My friend Gary was standing outside wearing a red shirt.

I *saw* a color and shape combo and shot blindly as he twisted around and wondered what was taking me so long.

I *didn't see* the girl with her billowing ball gown right away.

After I got it into the computer, I sensed an idea and saturated the color, heightened the contrast, and fiddled around as much as the ancient primitive photo program allowed.

Eventually it became this abstract metaphor: every little girl's Cinderella dream.

Badass.

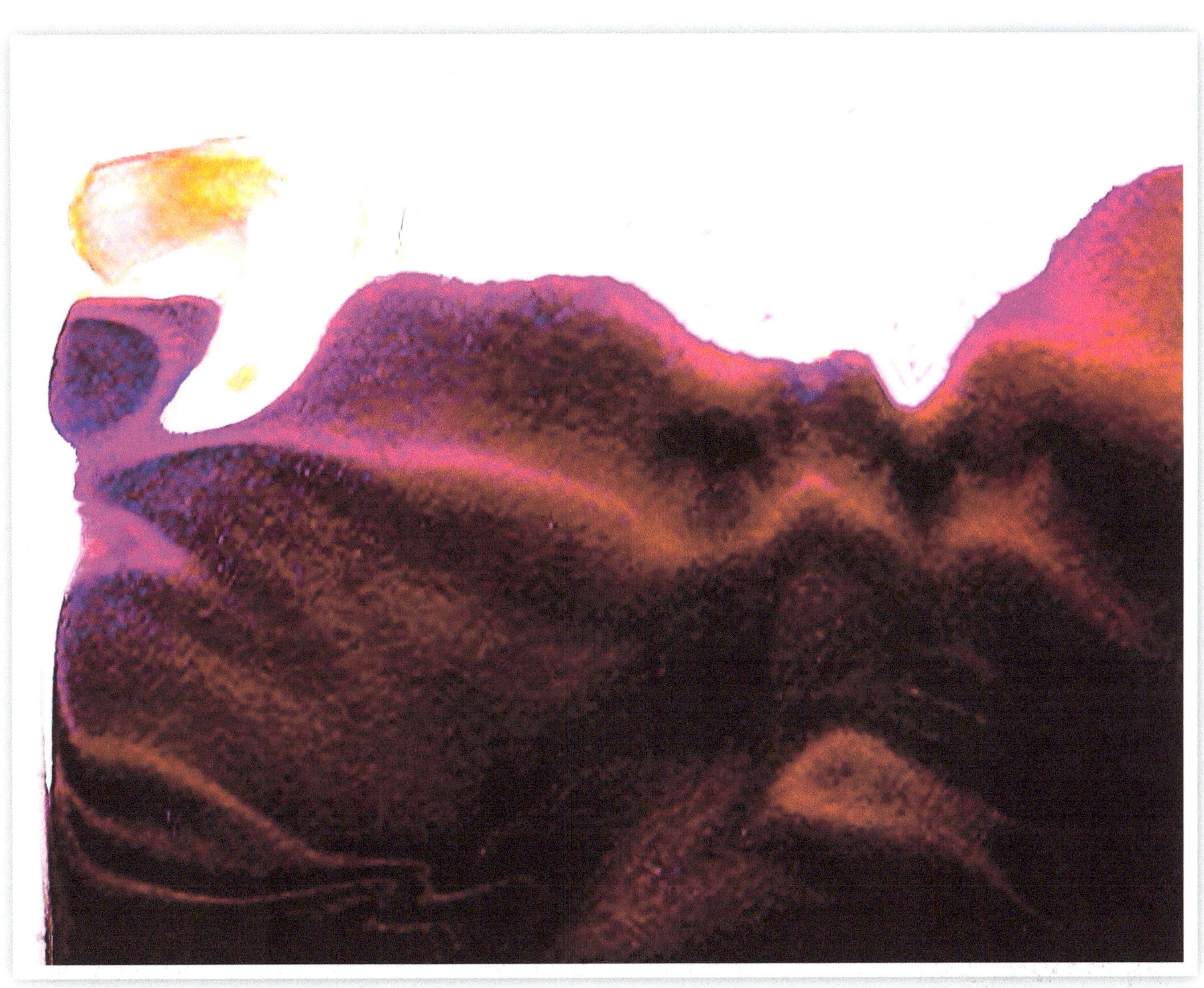

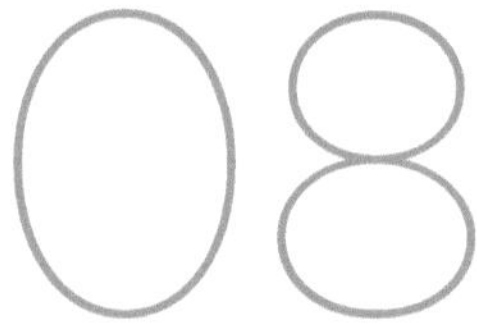

NARCISSUS, 2007

Another glass block, with a more complicated swirly pattern, and a denser background than Girl in Gown, although essentially the exact same technique. Shifting your gaze even an inch or two can create wildly different images.

Go.

Try it.

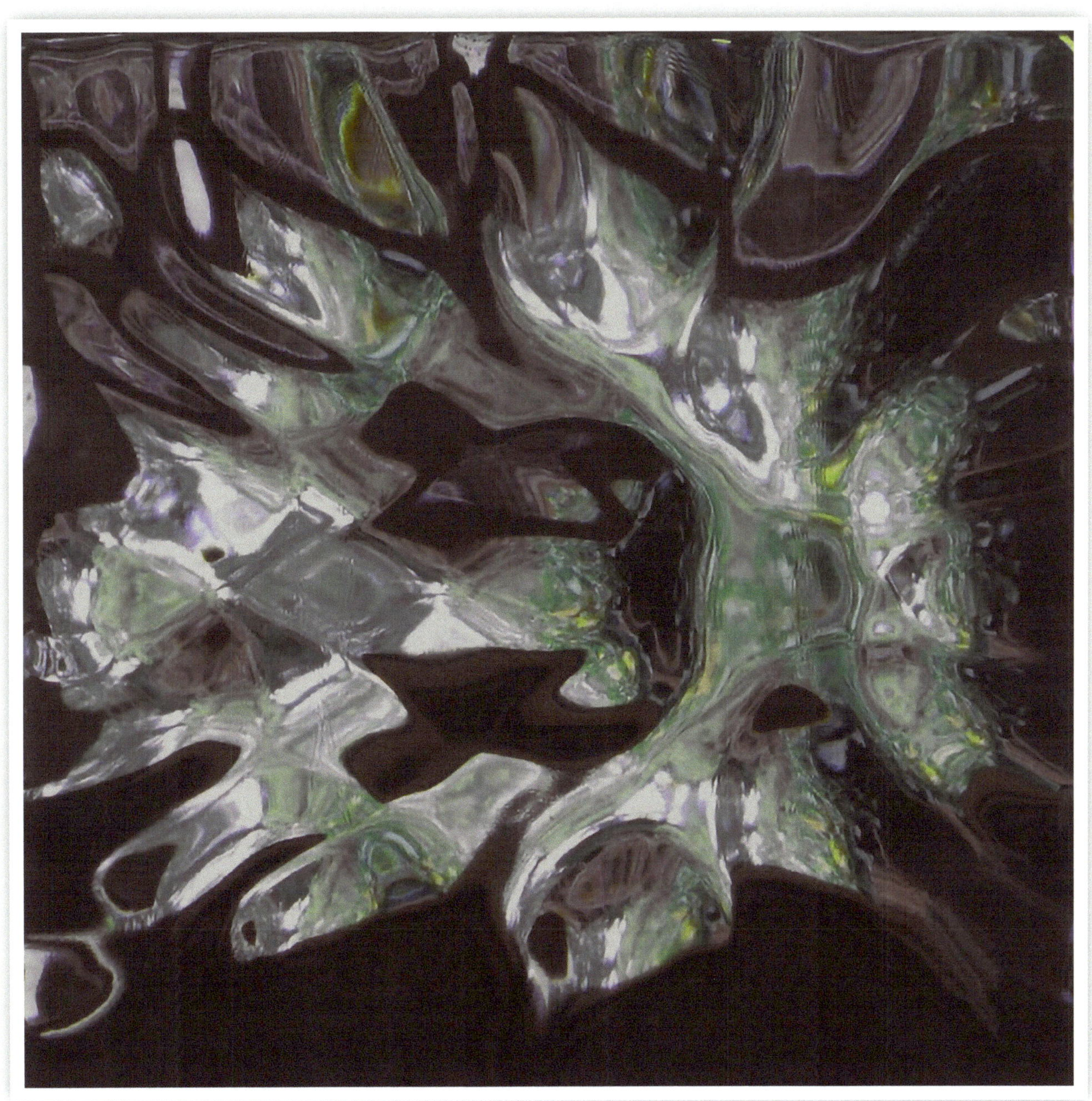

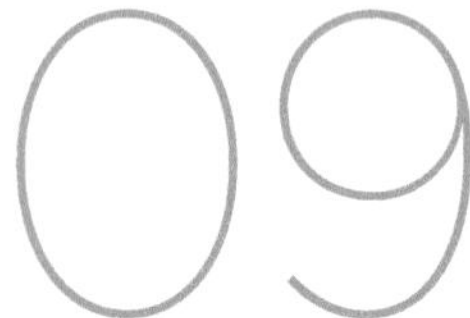

INTERSECTIONALITY, 2019

I was bike-riding around the neighborhood and came upon a smashed tv set on the sidewalk.

The iridescence in the sunlight was blinding and thrilling, as I angled myself all over it with my wimpy iPhone 6.

I eventually pedaled home, returned with my car, and shoveled the entire hunk of wreckage into the back seat. Strangely enough, it was impossible to recapture any of this magic with the lovely and talented (and cheap-ass) DSLR camera.

Go figure.

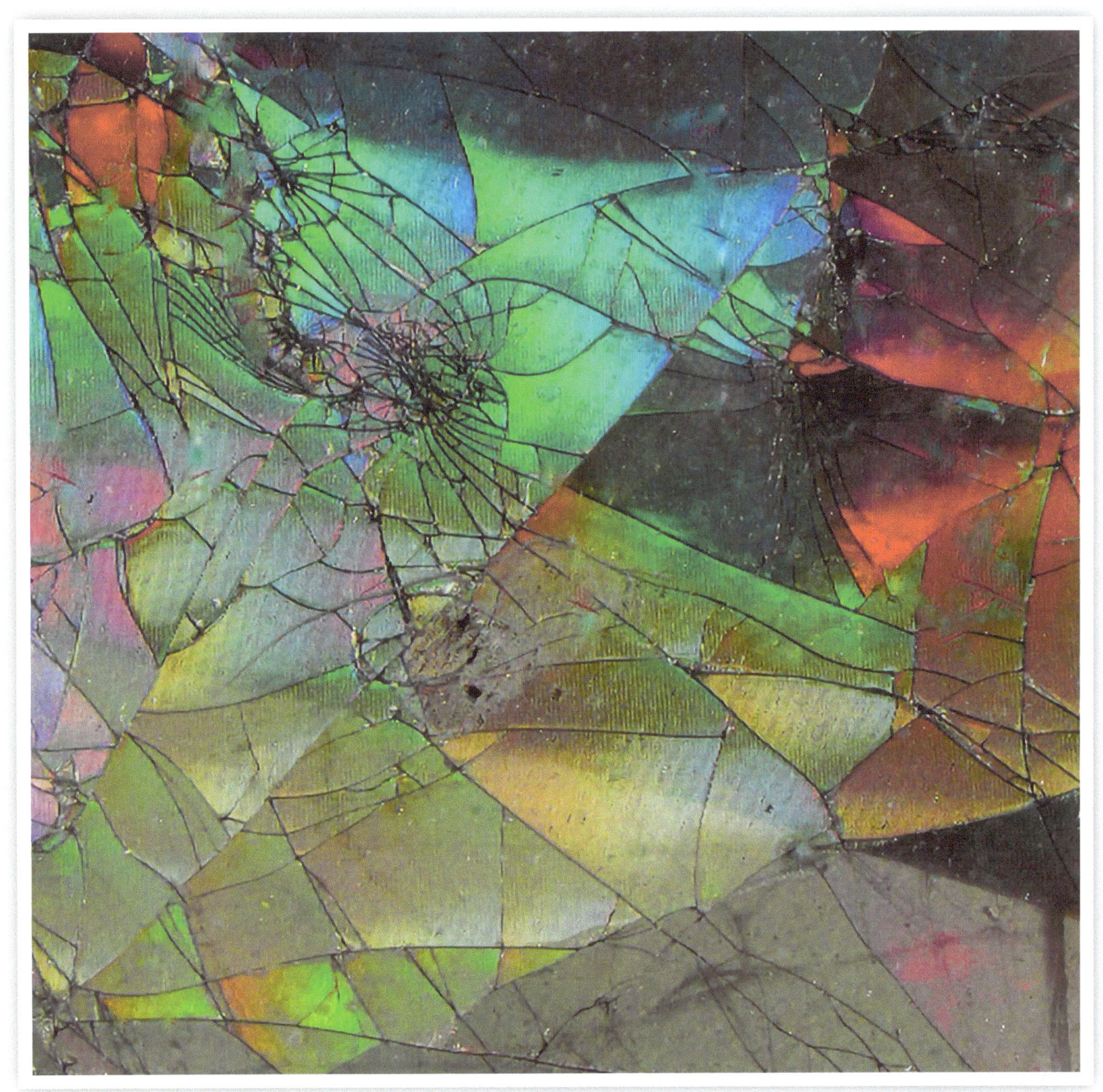

ART SECTION II: **CREATIVE VIEWPOINT**

In photography, the viewpoint is the position from which the shot is taken and will also be the place of the viewer as he/she sees the resulting picture. If you can't induce vertigo or seasickness or at least throw folks off their game, you aren't trying hard enough.

10. Mushroof

11. Skywest

12. Chicago Under Glass

13. Venus & Buddha

10

MUSHROOF, 2012

The miracle of the smart phone: it can get into the weensiest spaces and still focus!

I just slid it underneath the belly of this huge mushroom and shot, without seeing what I was aiming at.

Found out what I had afterwards: astonishment brought visual.

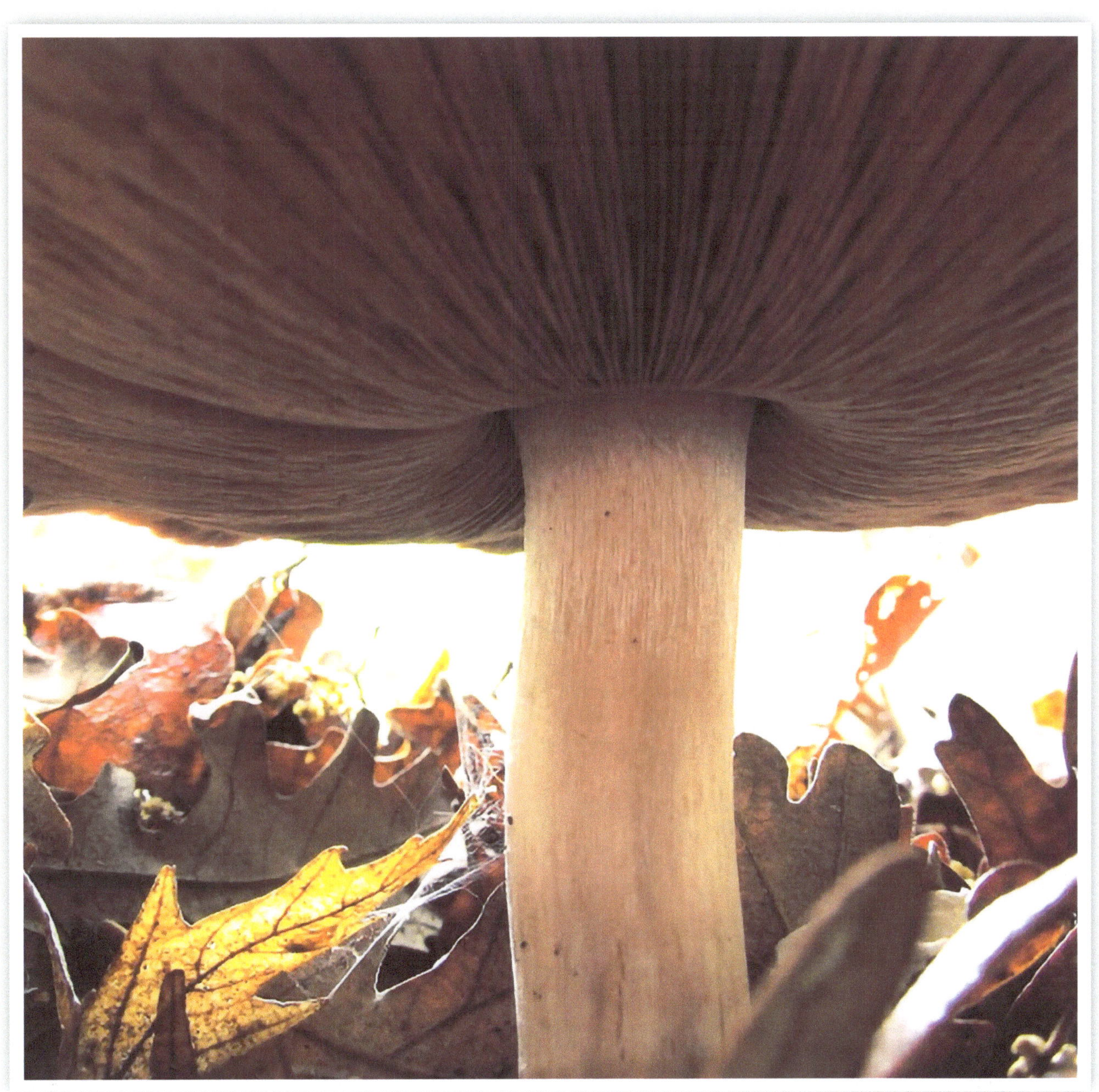

11

SKYWEST, 2009

I traveled on SkyWest Airlines only this once. At the time, they were flying the Embraer 120 Brasilia aircraft (pictured), which wasn't painted, but highly polished like stainless steel.

I got the first seat behind the cockpit. This image is the side of the airplane and the clouds below us, reflected on the engine housing in flight.

The other passengers thought I was batshit crazy, hunched into that tiny dusty oval window with the camera lens pushed up against the glass.

But it worked.

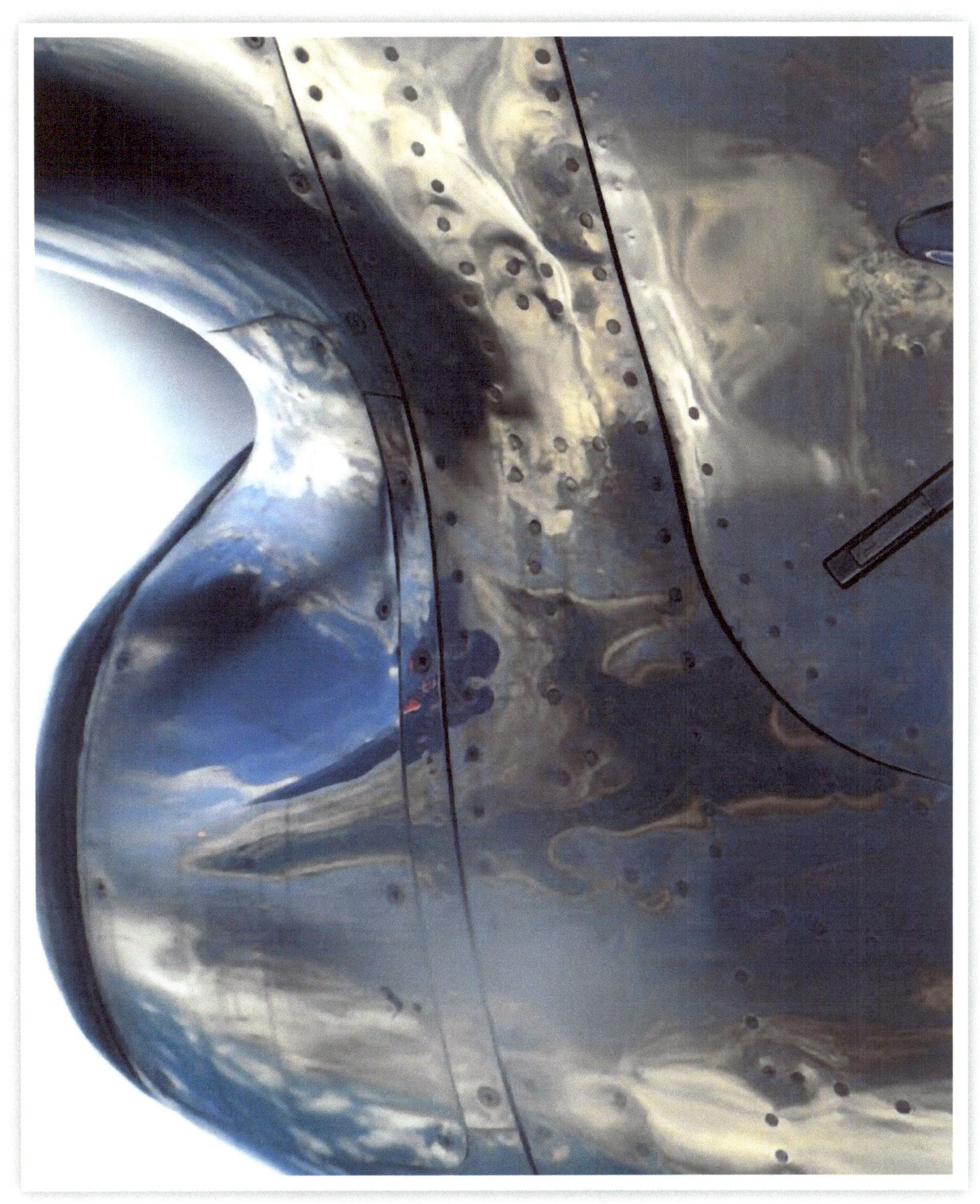

12

CHICAGO UNDER GLASS, 2011

Can't get a clear angle on a shot? Find something to reflect it.

This was taken from the 95th floor restaurant in the John Hancock building.

There were lots of beams and barriers and reassuring safety features up there; downside, they blocked out some interesting views.

Plus, I was with a group of new friends who might not have appreciated me clambering over their food and drinks to get a good photo. My regular homies would've pushed aside their plates and hoisted me up on their shoulders, but they were two time zones away and likely in their loungewear.

Lesson time: don't just make do, *make art,* with whatcha got.

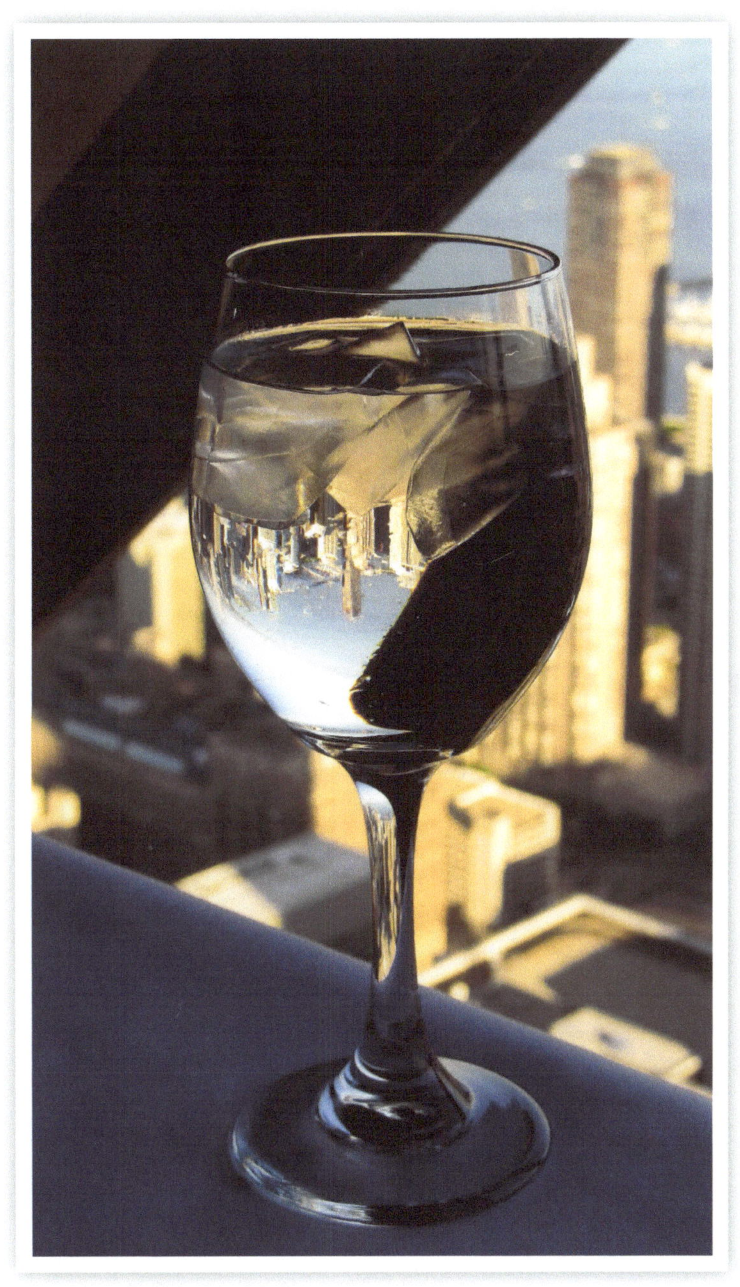

13

VENUS AND BUDDHA, 1996

The creative viewpoint here is a bit of staging and placement of the statues.

I visited my future mother-in-law's home and amused myself by repositioning them so Buddha's leer and Venus's sightline matched up, while making sure the viewer could experience the drama and sexual tension.

Further creative license: I hung up extra ivy vines (this is a film photo, and waaaay before Photoshop) to hide distracting flaws and keep the focus where it belonged.

By-the-by, this piece was kicked out of a show, *without* refund of my entry fee. Apparently (?) the judges were offended by a prudish nude and a laughing model of spiritual enlightenment in the same shot. *I am not making this shit up.*

But boy-o-boy, does getting expelled look hell-o-matic authentic on my Badass resumé.

Yeah...

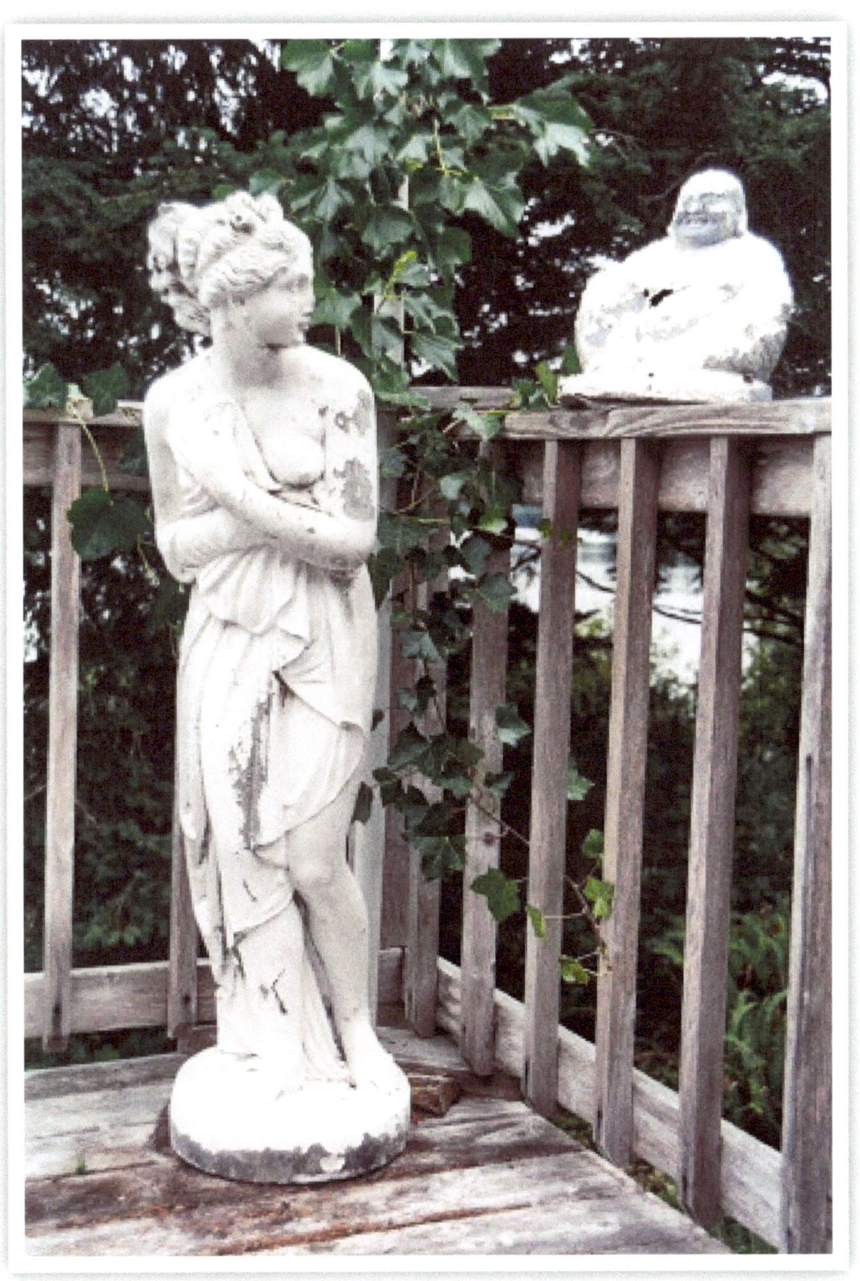

ART SECTION III: **ABSTRACTIONS**

A little deconstruction, a little distortion, a little scrambling of reality by various means.

Less talk.

More *see.*

14. Tiller

15. Whistler's Mother

16. Blue Gold

17. When the Levee Breaks

18. Bird in Winter Tree

19. Black Not Invisible

20. Race

21. I Wish I Had a River

22. Moonset: Port of Stockton

14

TILLER, 2011

During the magic hour (late afternoon, heading into dusk) I broke away from the party and made some Farm Art with my brother-in-law's tractor attachments.

Use of shadow and light obscures the real object.

And invites one of the most powerful forces in all of art, in all of creation: *human imagination*.

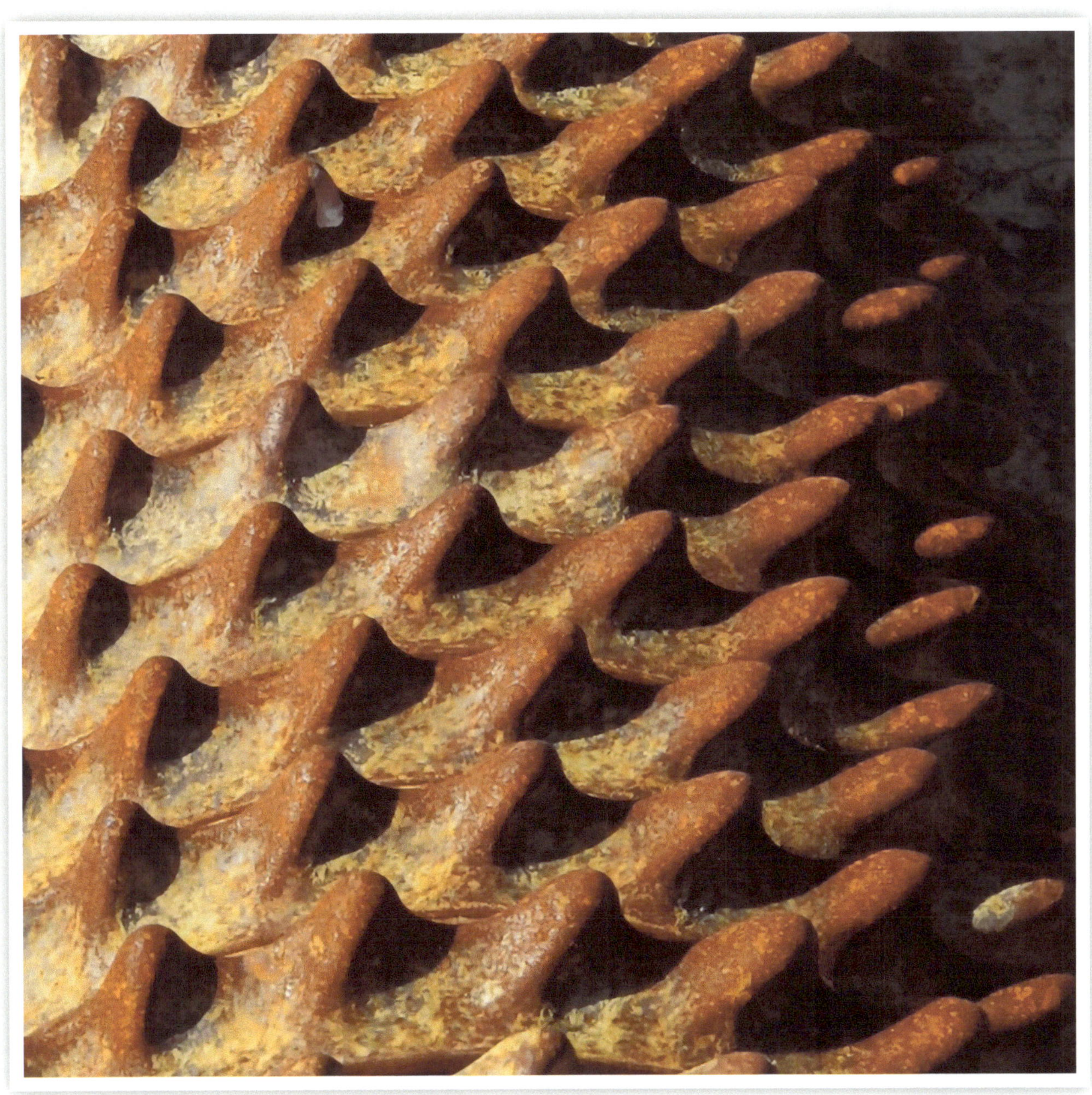

15

WHISTLER'S MOTHER, 2017

Deconstruction was already done.

I just showed up with a cheap-ass camera.

This is the side panel of a dumpster. One that had caught on fire. I saw a seated figure and a straight-back chair and had my title.

Finis.

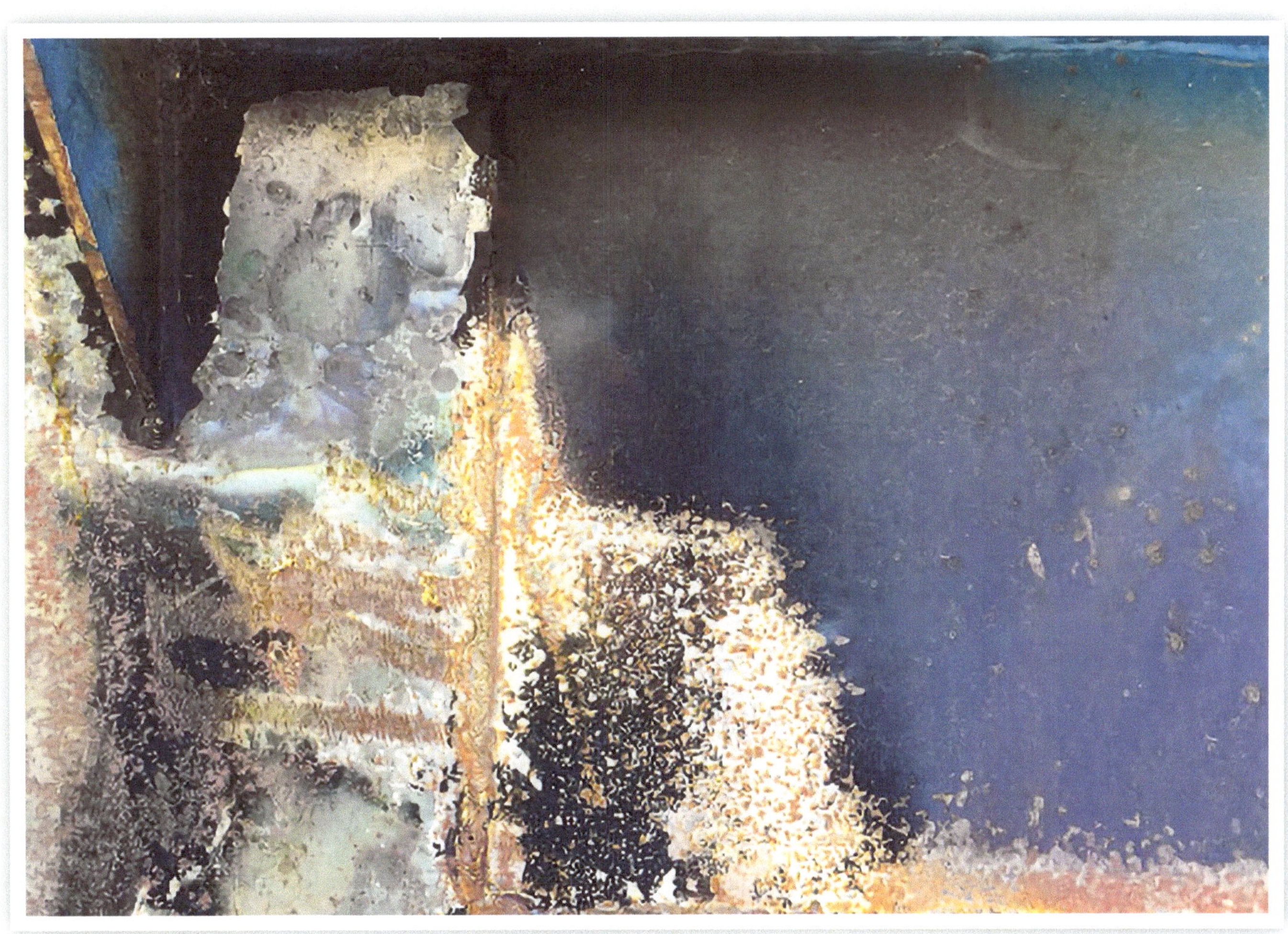

16

BLUE GOLD, 2018

Another cremated dumpster. Totally coincidental. I am not an arsonist.

May need to become or enlist one.

However[1].

1 Annie Mack is NOT suggesting that arson or property damage are proper activities. Please don't try them at home.

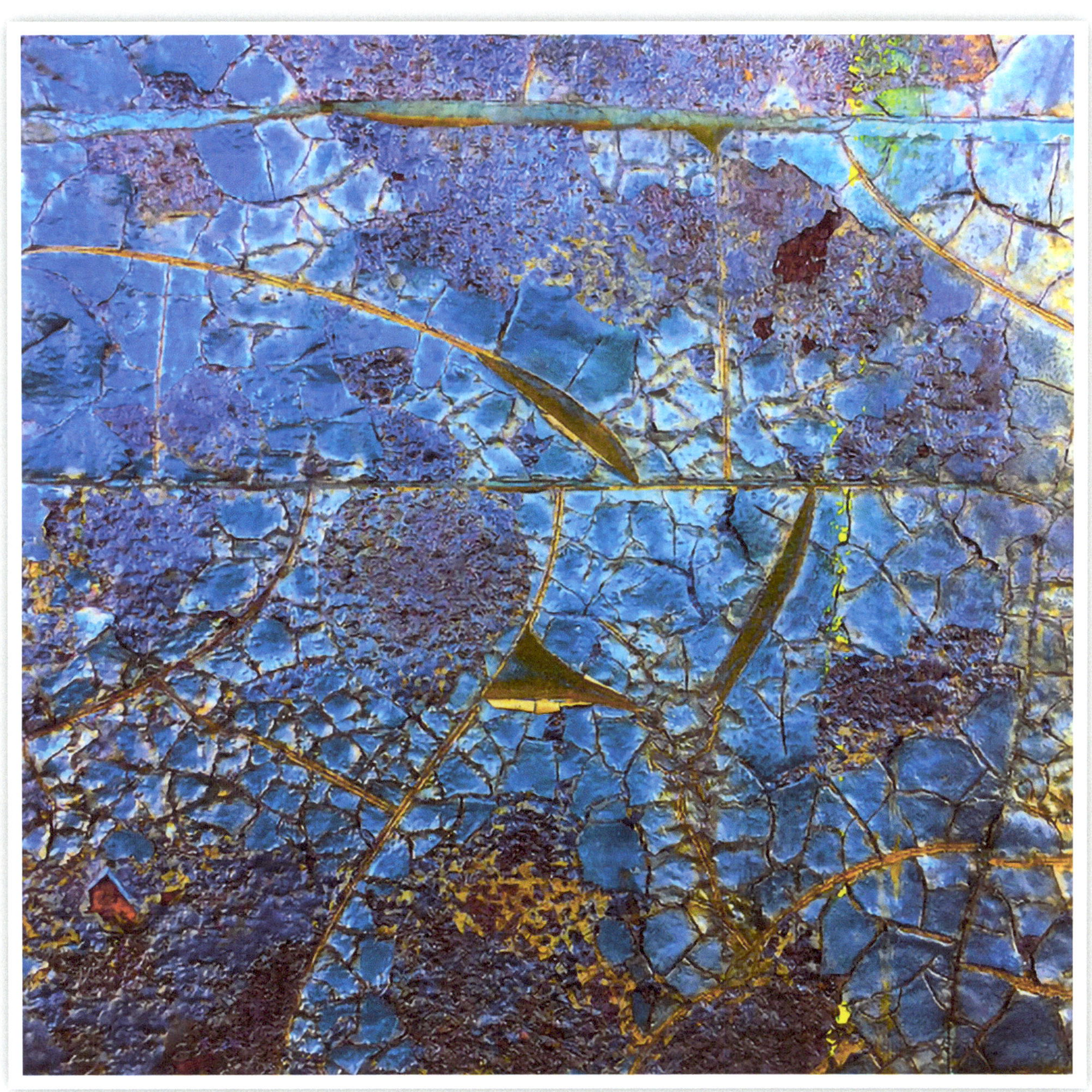

17

WHEN THE LEVEE BREAKS, 2018

OK, OK, OK!

Just one more.

"No, sir, officer. I did not set that dumpster ablaze for artistic purposes. I would never..."[2]

---

2 Annie Mack is...*yada-yada-yada* same-as-last-time.

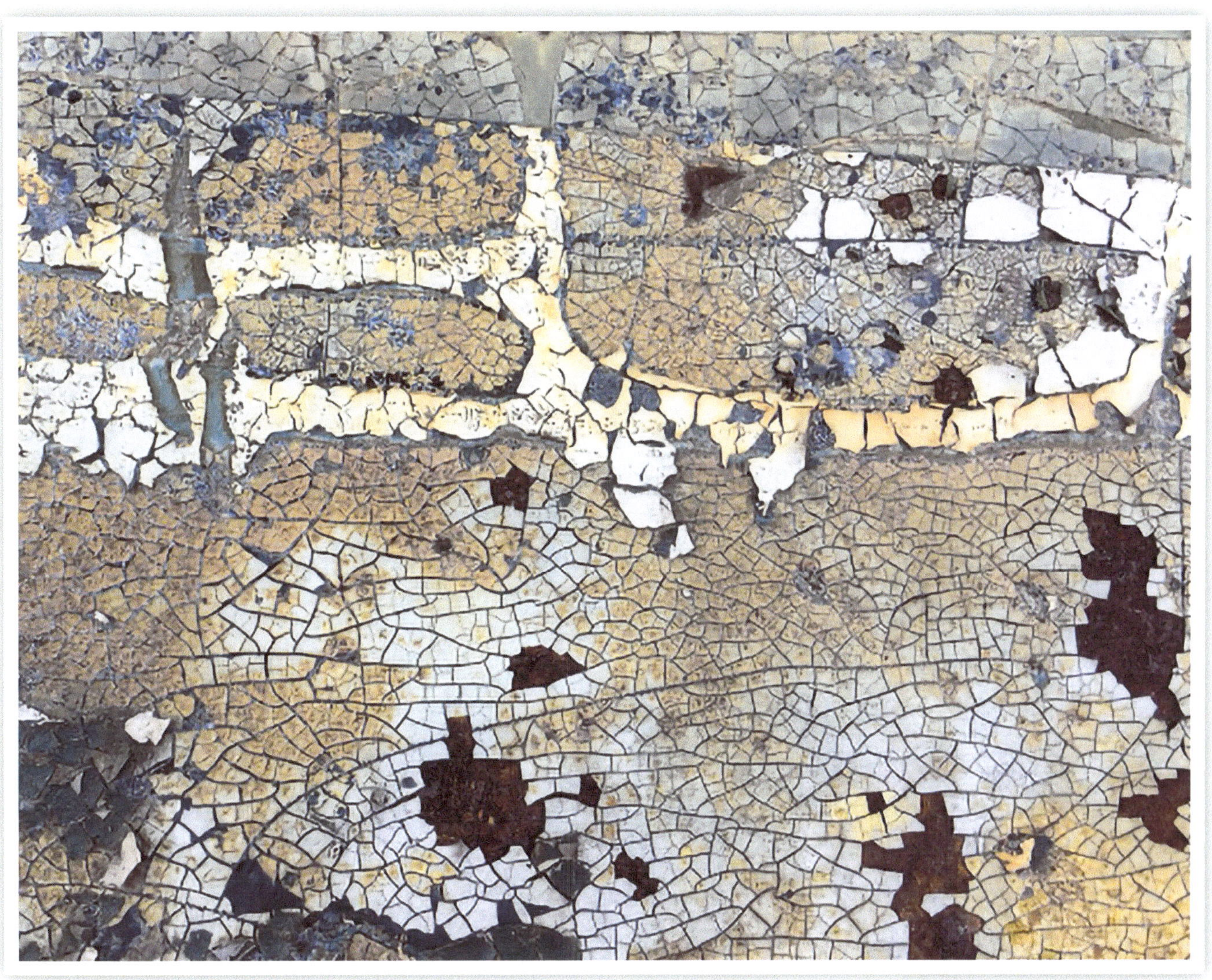

18

BIRD IN WINTER TREE, 2008

Before the badassery, this was “just” a rusted and dirty galvanized metal bucket.

An image shot in natural light will present the color spectrum’s tones when you punch up the hue and saturation in the computer.

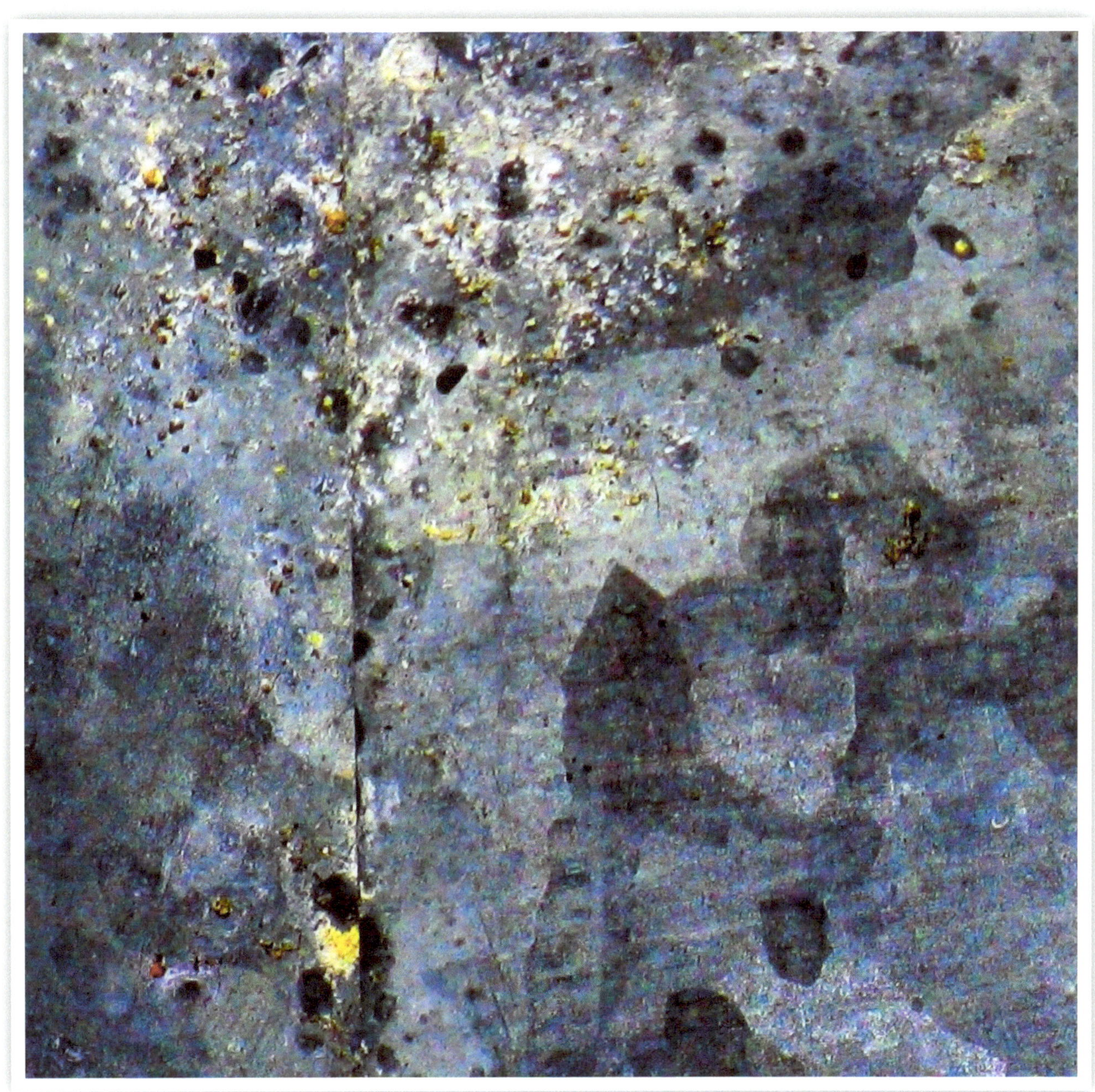

19

BLACK, NOT INVISIBLE, 2020

Art is a product of a reaction to the artist's emotional and chronological surroundings. I found this image during the height of Black Lives Matter protests and Shelter-in-Place during the COVID-19 crisis.

Whether or not to assign a title at all is a common dilemma for abstractionists.

A splashy caption can seem like fishing or trying too hard and comes off as self-aggrandized or desperate. A strong untitled piece can stir up audience feelings and questions without prompting.

But sometimes...

[3]a skillfully worded phrase...

puts it in a context...

that *magnifies*

its resonance

and

i m p a c t.

---

3 Meant to be read slow, like as if savoring a fine California Opus One Cabernet Sauvignon

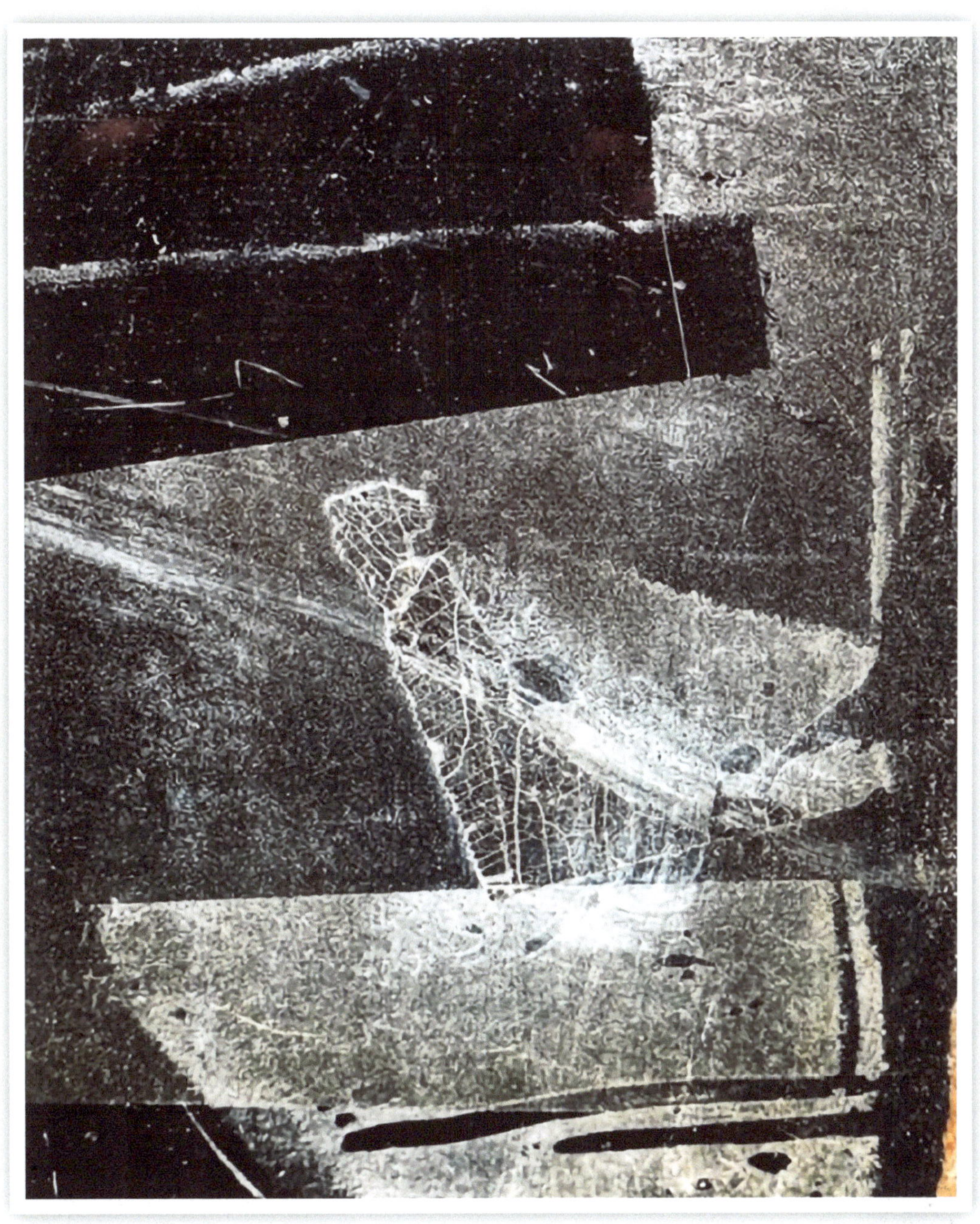

20

RACE, 2015

Race: the word's double meaning, and the image's contrasting elements,

created a metaphor for the

lack…

… of

social justice

in Black America.

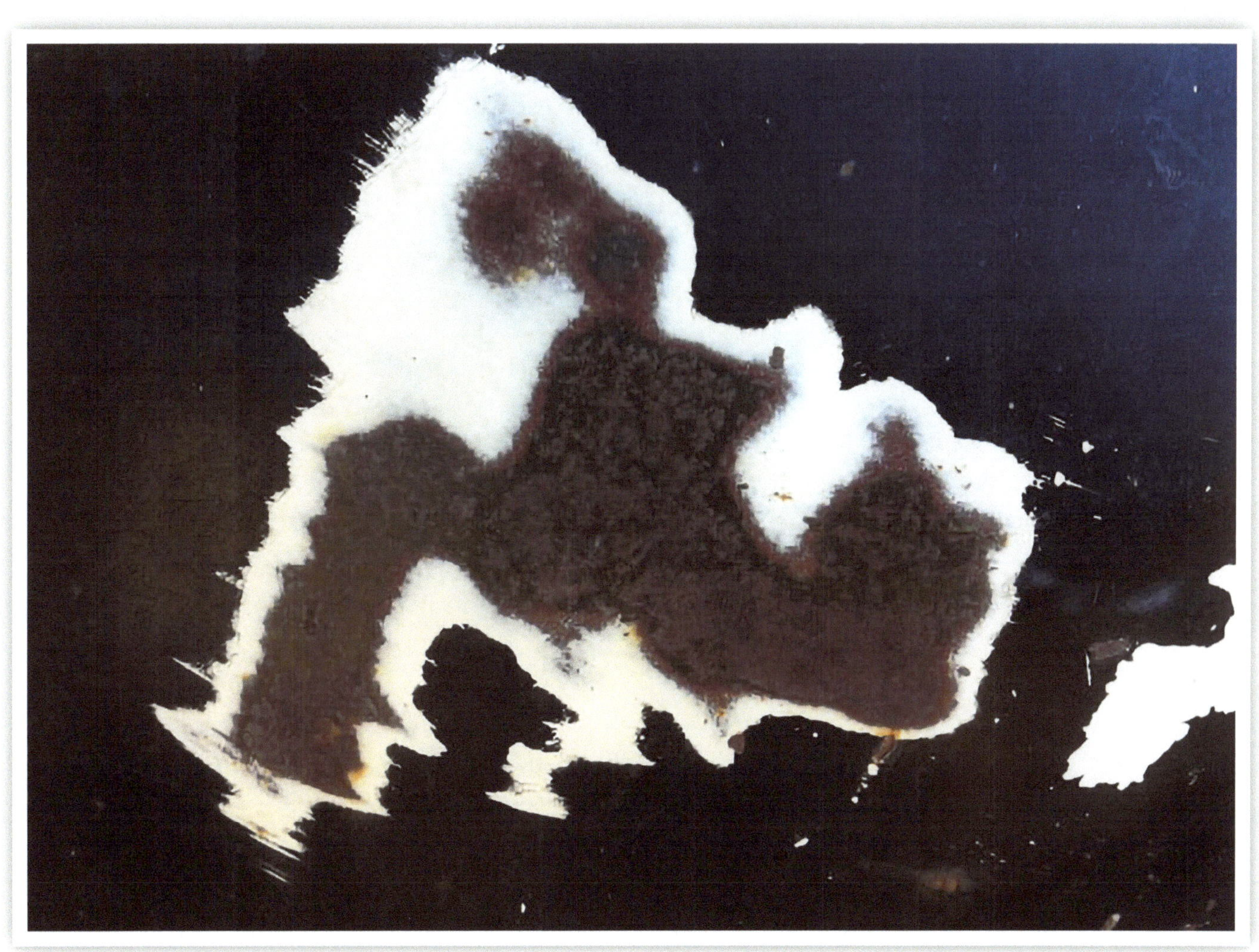

21

I WISH I HAD A RIVER, 2015

Fantasy abstract.

Original is a scraped and sanded fender of a 1951 Ford pickup.

I used the *Invert* function, which treats the image like those old film negatives, and reverses the color values (or whatever it is, you know what I mean).

In this parallel universe, the little skater leaped out in the dark and blue mood, and from there, it was a no-brainer homage to...

...Ms. Joni Mitchell.

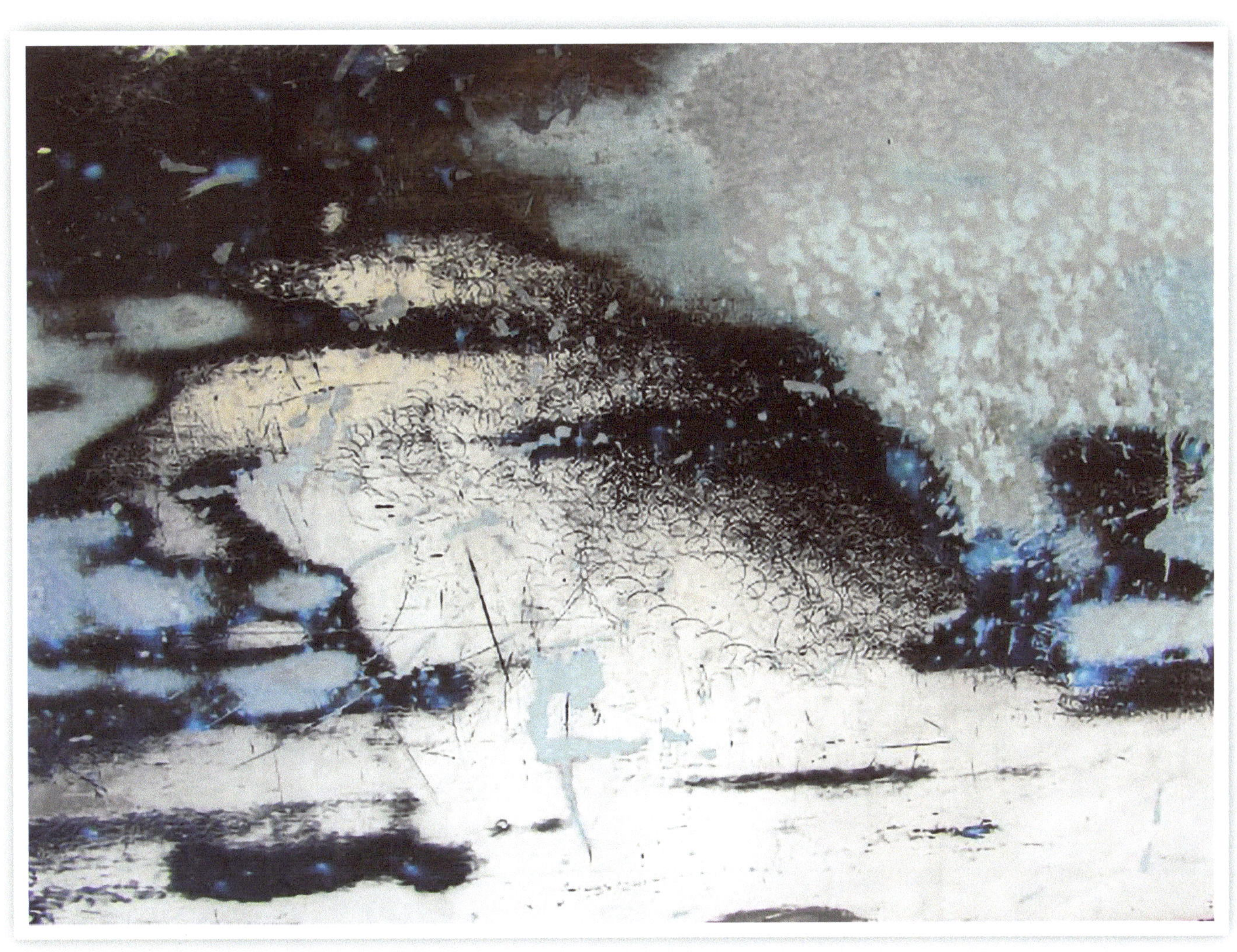

22

MOONSET: PORT OF STOCKTON, 2014

I already warned you about this. Long story short-ish: I was returning from the train station at 4 am, half-awake in a bathrobe, slippers, and wrong-prescription glasses, when I saw the moon setting behind a docked ship and some grain elevators.

I jumped out of the car and fumbled around (I couldn't see a damn thing) and tried to shoot before the moon sank below the skyline.

My cheap-ass camera "jammed," for lack of a better word for a stupid digital box that shouldn't be able to "jam" in the first place. I punched the button wildly in the hope that it would fix itself and start focusing.

It recorded without fixing until I got it home.

Moral of the story: Faulty cameras can produce beautiful bokeh.

Extra Credit Homework: Guess which one is the moon.

ART SECTION IV: **MACROS**

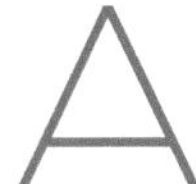

s I said in the intro, photography macro shots often become abstracts when the subject is cropped beyond recognition.

23. Heart of Glass, 2018

24. Untitled (Black), 2014

25. Galaxies in Collision, 2019

26. Cold Harbor, 2019

23

HEART OF GLASS, 2018

This picture captured the inside of a candle holder made of stained-glass grouted pieces.

The black heart is a bonus flaw, a vivid symbol among the hard-to-identify elements.

A theme within the mystery.

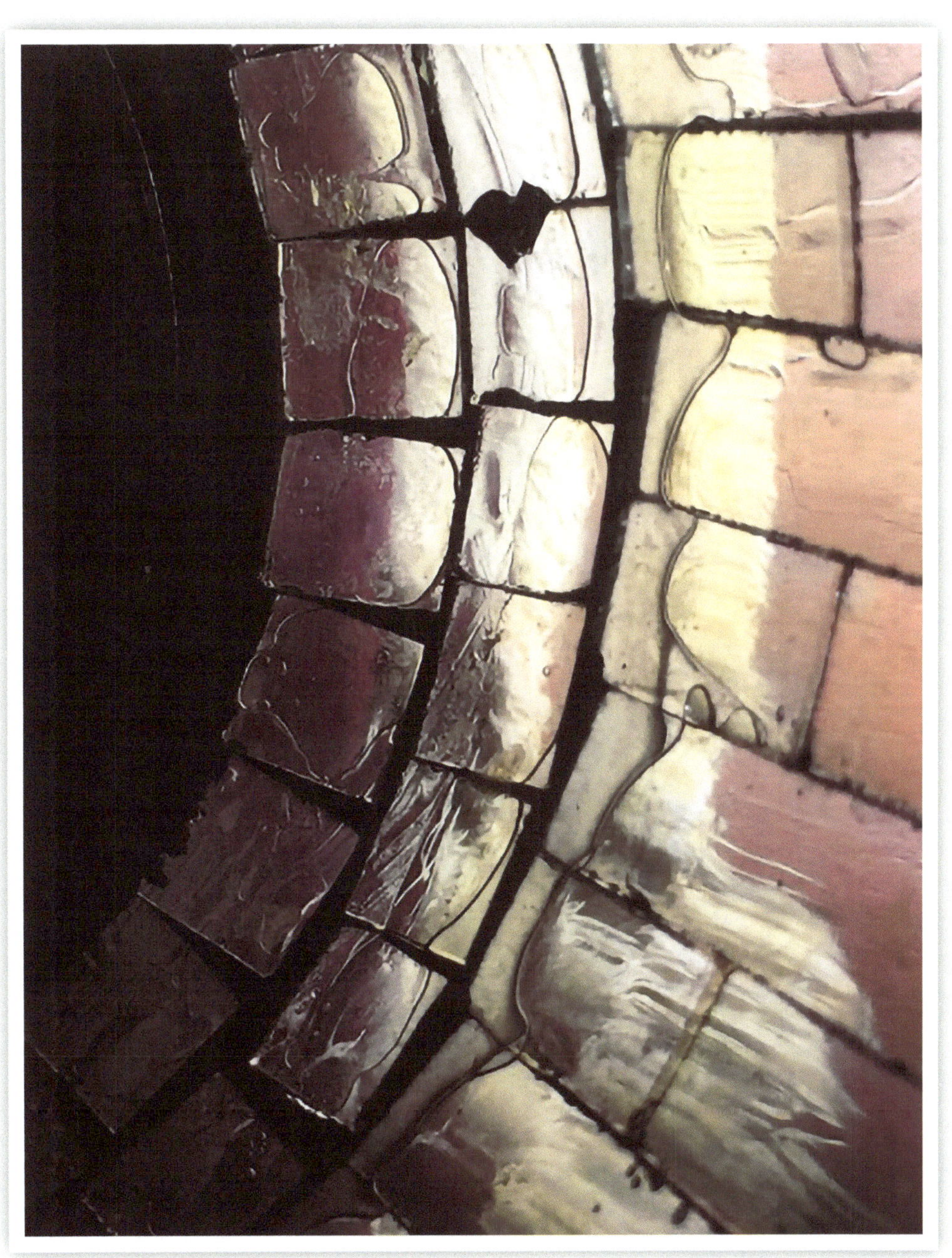

24

UNTITLED (BLACK), 2014

An enormous mushroom.

Upended,

And dehydrated,

In chilly temperatures.

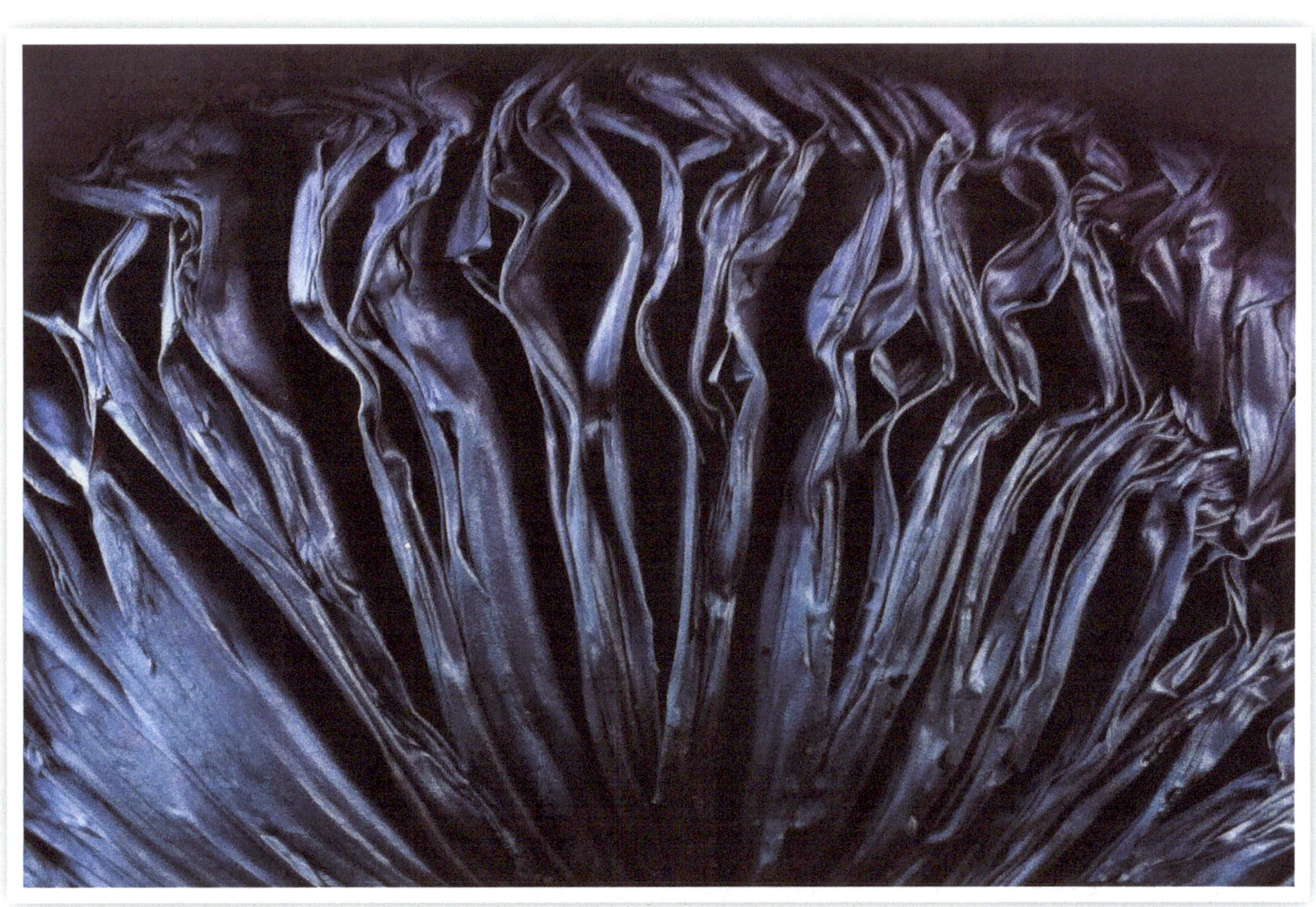

25

GALAXIES IN COLLISION, 2019

This work captures someone's amateurish attempt to fix a minor dent without proper tools.

Fantastic art, though!

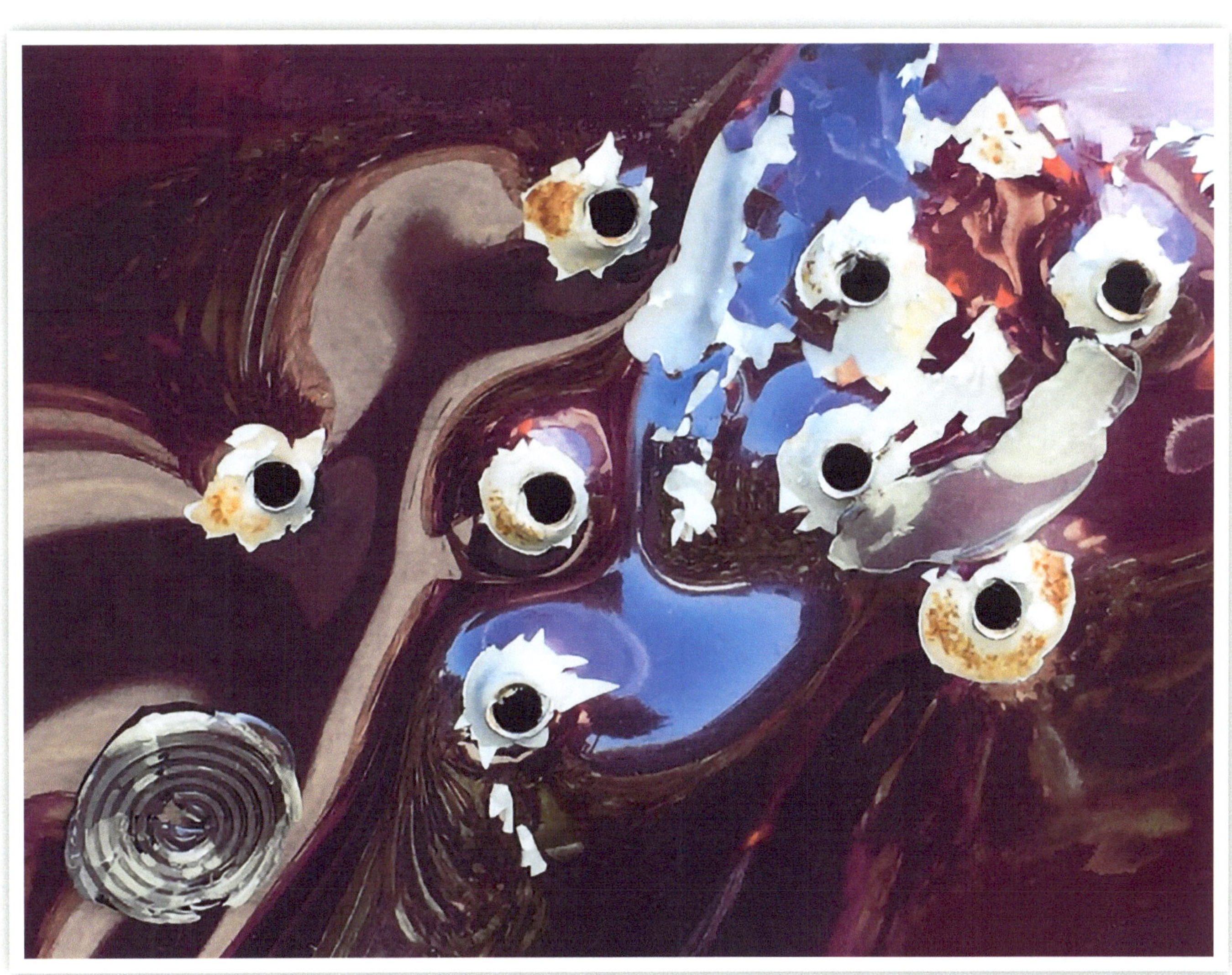

26

COLD HARBOR, 2019

The power of suggestion is mighty.

I shot this in a sweltering hot asphalt parking lot.

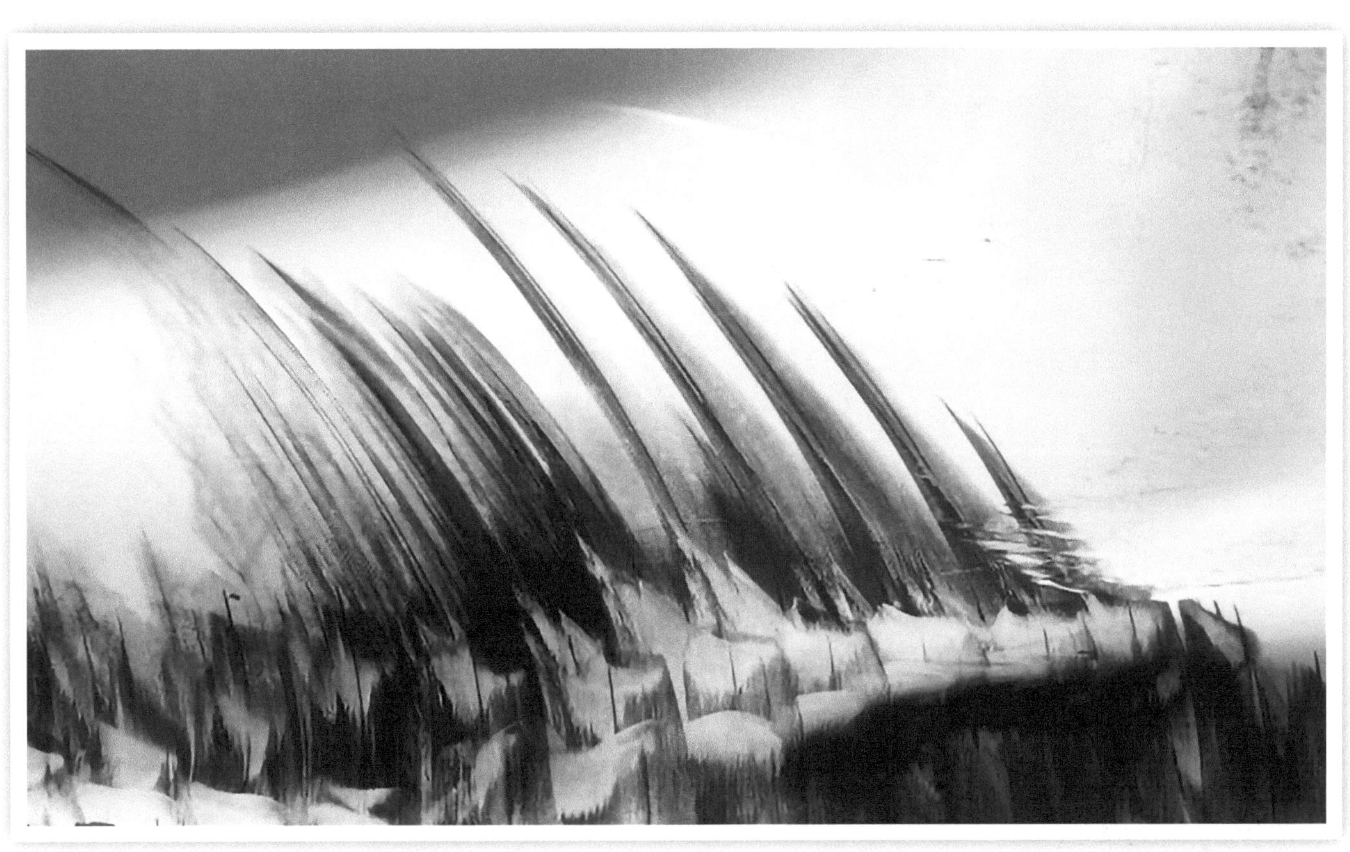

ART SECTION V: **FORTUITOUS MOMENTS**

Time. Ever expanding, but always...*now*.

How to capture it?

Luck. Ineffable. You can feel it when it happens.

Necessary.

Awareness. Focus. Patience.

Practiced.

Breathe...

And a cheap-ass camera.

When all of those above intersect it can lead to a fortuitous moment.

Like these.

27. City Lights

28. Parkland 17

29. Shadows of the Eclipse

30. Concert on the Waterfront

27

CITY LIGHTS, 2007

A fancy-ass setup might've captured this in detail.

And missed all the *fantastic* magic.

Cheap-ass for the win!

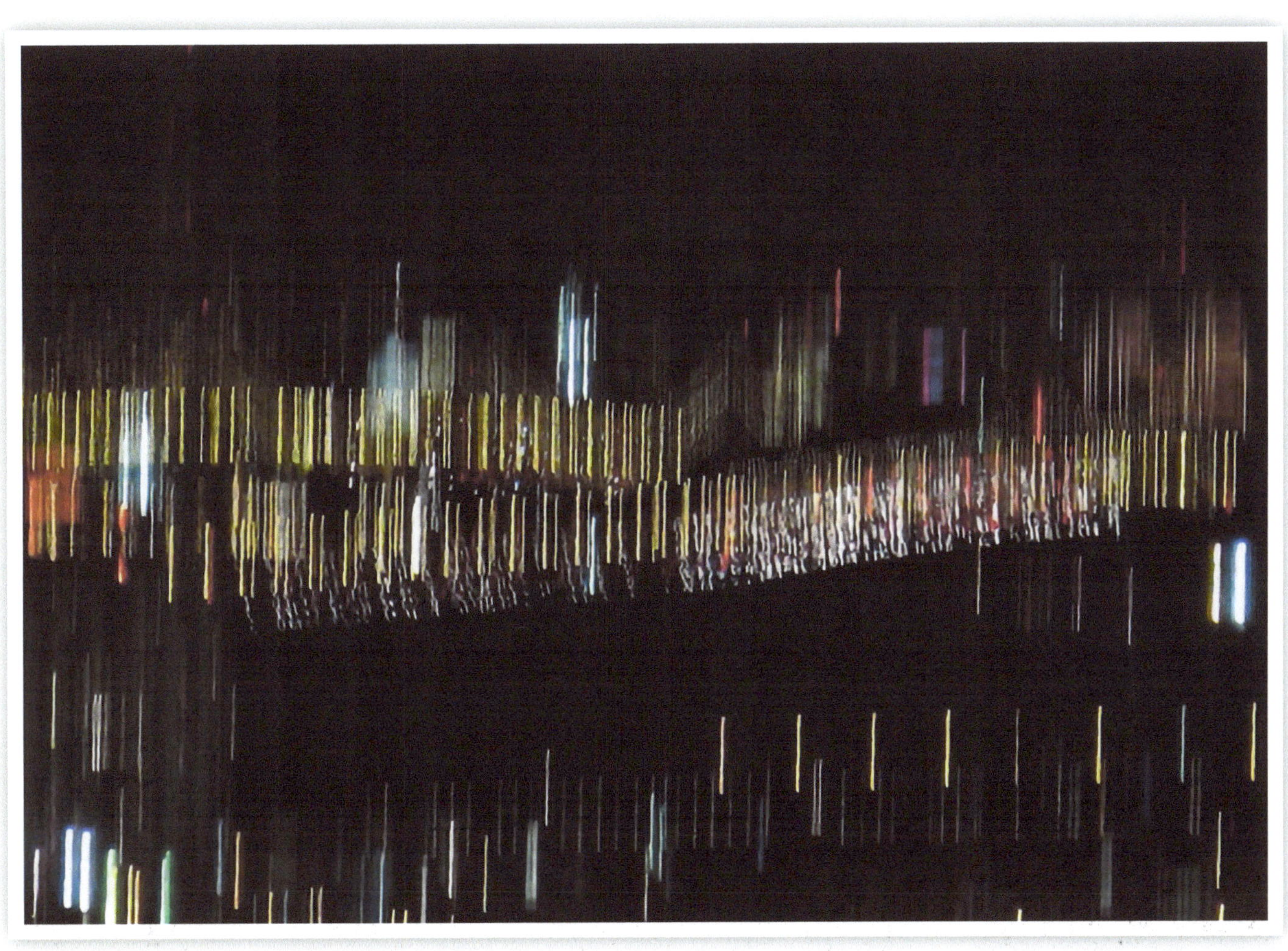

28

PARKLAND 17, 2018

Student activists in Florida organized nationwide protests following the school shootings at Marjory Stoneman Douglas High School.

I marched with my local group.

The crosswalk alert was inadvertently captured at 17...

...the number of Parkland victims.

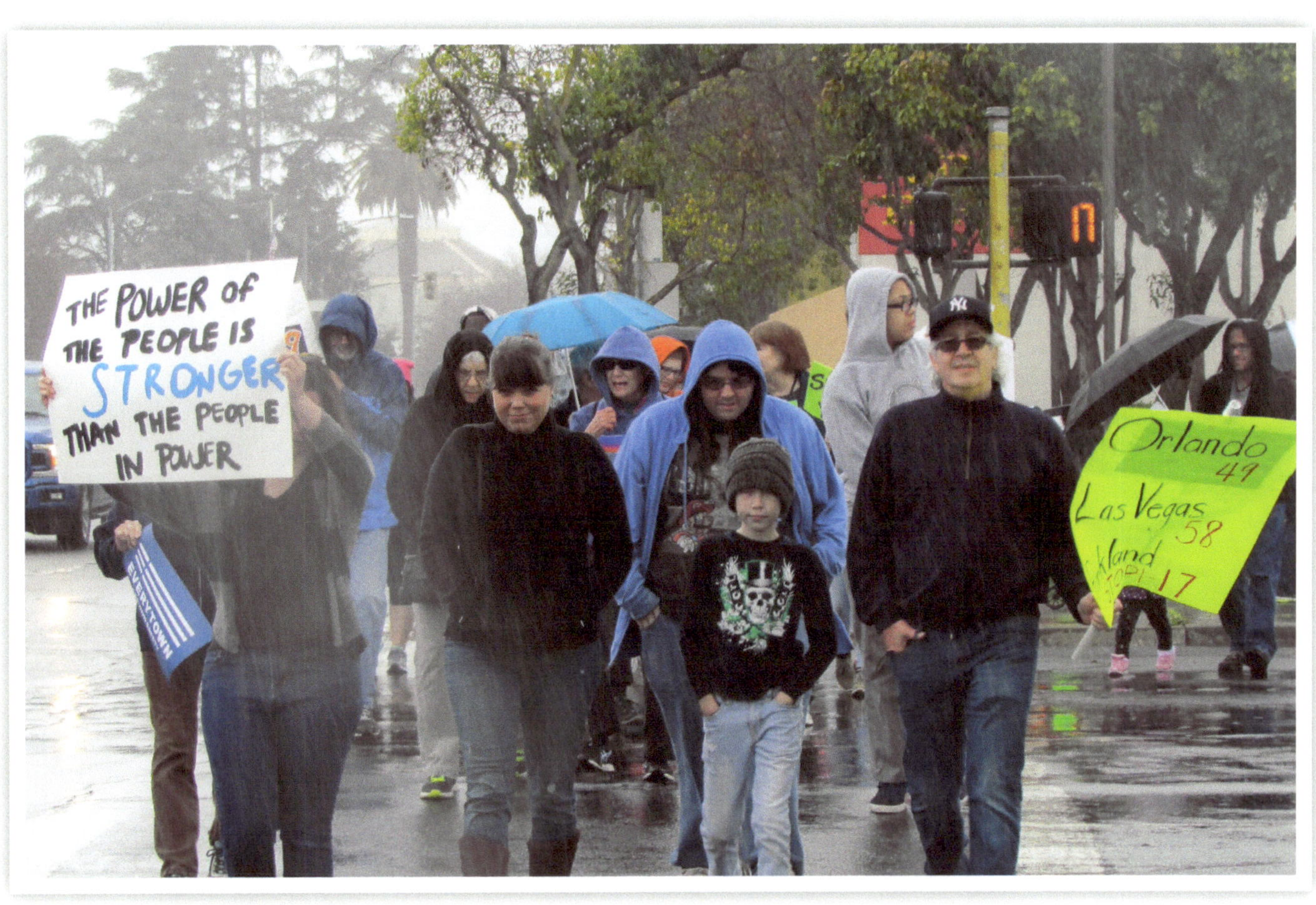
THE POWER OF THE PEOPLE IS STRONGER THAN THE PEOPLE IN POWER
EVERYTOWN
Orlando 49
Las Vegas 58
17

29

SHADOWS OF THE ECLIPSE, 2012

This work captures sunlight during a solar eclipse shining through the trees onto the garage door.

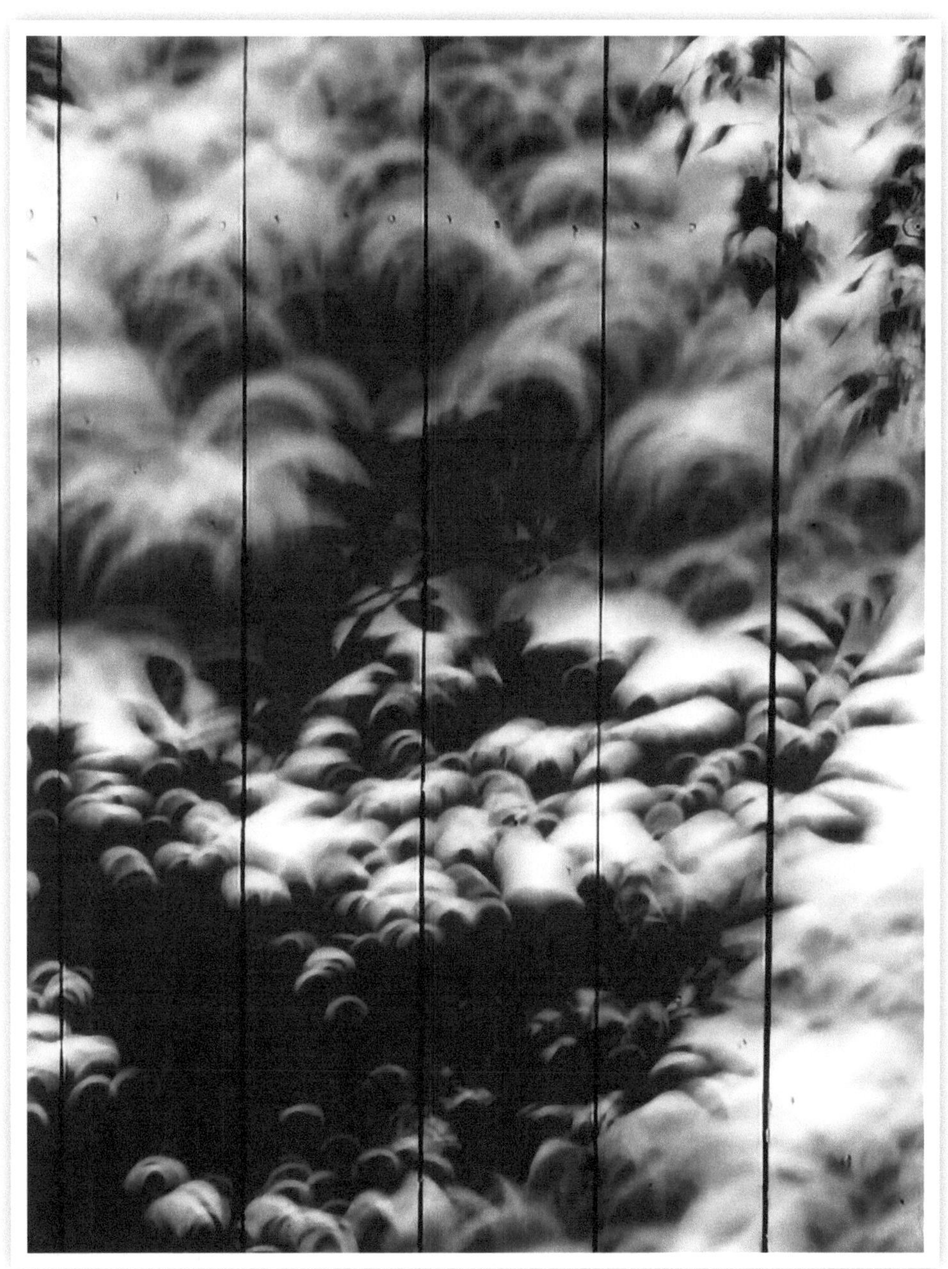

30

CONCERT ON THE WATERFRONT, 2007

A handy tip from the amateur's handbook: "If you don't have a tripod, set the camera on a stable structure with a level surface."

And little musical notes will appear.

Hey, thanks!

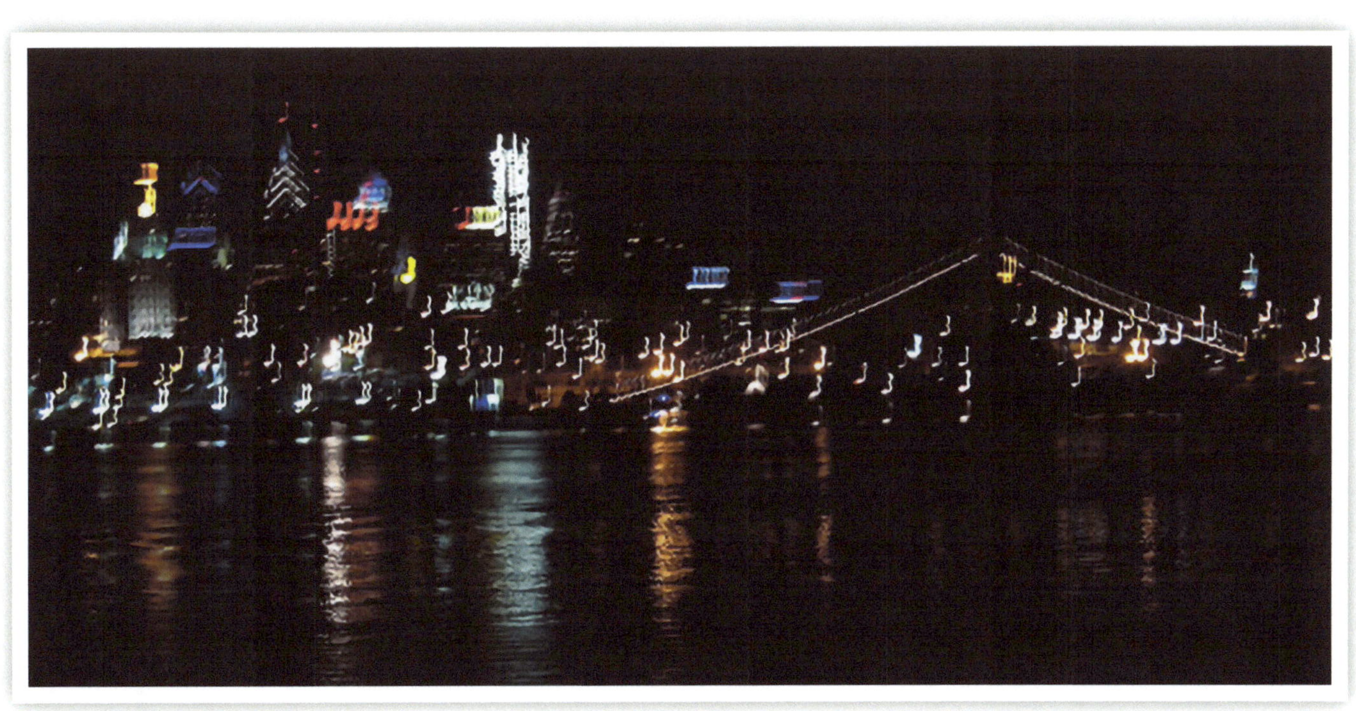

EPILOGUE

I hope you have been inspired, encouraged, or irritated enough to go be Badass your own self.

Prove me right.

Or wrong.

But have a good time.

—Annie

REFERENCES / FOOTNOTES

- Hasselblad reference in the introduction: *https://www.bhphotovideo.com/c/product/1384729-REG/hasselblad_h_3013775_h6d_400c_multi_shot_medium_format.html*
- 2nd Street Tunnel: Clifford Oto's comments, published: April 5, 2014, The Record, Stockton, CA.
- Walt Disney Concert Hall, from *Wikipedia*: Plans were revised. The initially designed stone exterior was replaced with a less costly stainless steel skin in a cost-saving move.
- Types of photography (Reflection) *https://showme.co.za/pretoria/lifestyle/photography/photography-categories-types-of-photography/*
- Annie Liebowitz: *https://www.masterclass.com/classes/annie-leibovitz-teaches-photography*
- Creative Viewpoint definition: The viewpoint refers to the position we take a photograph from. This will also be the viewer's position when they are looking at your finished shot. The viewpoint can dramatically change the feel of the picture. One example of this is the American Street photographer William Klein. Mar 29, 2012 Composition - The Viewpoint - The Photographic Angle *https://www.thephotographicangle.co.uk* — June 29, 2020.
- SkyWest unpainted plane: *https://www.airportspotting.com/skywest-retires-embraer-120/* June 29, 2020.
- Chicago Under Glass: *https://en.wikipedia.org/wiki/John_Hancock_Center*

- Moonset: Port of Stockton: it's the dark yellow circle on the far right.
- Galaxies in Collision: thanks to Lon Baugh, Atwater Automotive, proprietor, for technical advice.
- City Lights: Looking southwestward from the Berkeley hills to San Francisco.
- Parkland 17: *https://www.history.com/this-day-in-history/parkland-marjory-stoneman-douglas-school-shooting*
- Concert on the Waterfront: skyline of Philadelphia.

Notes

Notes

Notes

Notes

Notes

www.ingramcontent.com/pod-product-compliance
Lightning Source LLC
LaVergne TN
LVHW070132110826
845147LV00002B/234
9781735413525